The Grail Quest

Search for Transcendence

By

Earle de Motte

First published in Australia in 2003 by the
Rosicrucian Order AMORC,
Grand Lodge for Australia, Asia and New Zealand

P.O. Box 1087
Burwood North NSW 2134
Australia

ABN 95 072 728 968

National Library of Australia
Cataloguing-in-Publication Data
De Motte, Earle
The Grail Quest: Search for Transcendence
ISBN: 1 876965 002

Printed in Australia
Typeset by the Rosicrucian Order AMORC
Cover painting by Alan Thurman
Cover design by McCauley Creative

Contents

Preface 4

Introduction: Symbolism of the Holy Grail 6

1 The Grail as a Miraculous Object 9

2 A Stone Falls from Heaven 15

3 Grail Guardians 21

4 The Home of the Grail 29

5 Mysteries and the Grail 38

6 The Grail Alchemy 46

7 Symbols and Archetypes of the Grail Quest 53

8 Fisher King and Waste Land 62

9 The Goddess and the Grail 72

10 A Dark Side of the Myth 79

11 Further Horizons 87

12 Psychological and Mystical Perspectives 101

Appendix 1 The Shaping of the Grail Myth 110

Appendix 2 Primary Works on the Grail Quest 135

Appendix 3 Mons Philosophorum 137

Bibliography 143

Index 146

Preface

History's great legends enshrine truths which are of the utmost importance to us today. The secret wisdom of the ages has always been hidden in myths and legends. It is as if higher beings poured knowledge in symbolic form through those who could hear and record the great stories.

In the words of Sir George Trevelyan: "Every great myth, every great fairy tale, every great drama, and all epic poetry, is concerned with the symbol of the *hero* who undergoes some initiatory experience. Interpreting the scenario we must understand the setting to be symbolic of our whole personality, and the characters to portray the various aspects of it".

From the late Middle Ages the Grail symbol has occupied a special place in the Western imagination. The legend of the Grail is one of the archetypal myths that reveals a vital, healing, and uplifting message for our time, and it continues to exert a fascination upon all who come within its sphere of influence.

In the Arthurian legends the Grail and its Quest were intertwined with heroic tales of the Knights of the Round Table. Sir Galahad was the peerless knight of King Arthur's Round Table. He was the only knight chosen to sit in the "Siege Perilous" — a special seat at Arthur's great table reserved for him alone who should achieve the Quest of the Holy Grail.

At a feast the knights see a vision of the Grail which appears in the centre of the Round Table, but soon disappears. The knights then decide to take up the task of finding the missing Grail which they are told can only be recovered by the most morally perfect knight, who would then sit in the scat of honour — the "Siege Perilous."

The Grail, we are told, was invisible to all save him who was perfectly pure in thought, word, and deed; and its discovery would bring great wisdom, protection in battle, and constantly renewed life to the person possessing it.

In *Parzival* by Wolfram von Eschenbach, the 12th century German epic poet and minnesinger, the hermit Trevrizent explains to the Grail Knight that the Grail cannot be won by striving and achievement in the material world, but only through love, compassion, and letting go:

"I mourned for thy fruitless labour
For ne'er did the story stand
That the Grail might by man be conquered.
And I fain had withheld thine hand;
But with thee hath the chance been other,
And thy prize shall the highest be."

Beyond the guise of an earthly search by a noble knight for a lost Grail, there is a much deeper, more profound and mystical meaning to the Grail legend, for here is a profound allegory of mystical initiation, best and most completely understood by sincere students of Rosicrucian and related philosophies.

Robin M. Thompson, F.R.C.

This book is dedicated to Ailsa

Symbolism of the Holy Grail

By Ralph M. Lewis, F.R.C.(Past Imperator, Rosicrucian Order)

A combination of legend, romance, and mysticism surrounds the Holy Grail. The most familiar use of the words Holy Grail applies to the legendary cup used by Christ at the Last Supper. There seems to be, however, greater literary support for the interpretation which relates that the Grail was a vessel in which Joseph of Arimathea collected blood from the wounds of the Master Jesus. In these legends the Grail sometimes appears as a platter; in fact, there are many variations in its meaning. In the most authentic sources, the word is related to the Latin *crater*, or cup.

It was during the fifty year period of AD 1170—1220 that the great body of the romance about the Grail came into existence. However, it was not until as recently as 1861 that texts about the Grail began to appear. Most of these texts were thirteenth and fourteenth century transcriptions of a twelfth century manuscript by Chrétien de Troyes. The majority of the stories about the Grail were based on ancient myths. This resulted in there being four different heroes in the accounts: Perceval, Gawain, Bors, and Galahad — who was probably a later invention. It is thought that Galahad was invented by Walter Map as possibly a tribute to the son of Henry II.

It is related that the Grail was brought to England by Josephes, the son of Joseph, or by Brons, Joseph's brother in law. The legend states that the Grail was handed down from generation to generation and was thought to possess many mystical properties. One account tells of its being used to feed a multitude who were without sin by the means of multiplying a few loaves of bread so that they fed 500. Those who were not pure and who looked upon the Grail were struck dumb.

Reference to Perceval, one of the heroes associated with the tale of the Grail, states that he lived in seclusion from the royal court and was therefore kept in ignorance of chivalry. One day he came upon several knights and for the first time "seeing the splendour of their armour took them for angels." Subsequently, the legend continues, Perceval, Gawain, Bors, and Galahad set out upon a quest for the Grail. Though a number of the knights of King Arthur's court are related to have gone upon the journey, it was Galahad who was given the leading role in the quest. They are said to have sought for the Grail in the Far East. Galahad's soul was borne up to heaven by a great multitude of angels. Perceval died in a hermitage and Bors returned to Britain.

The Grail as Initiator

There have been, as said, many interpretations of the romance of the Grail which is principally thought to be an allegory expounding certain moral precepts. There is also the *initiation theory.* This is said to be similar to certain of the tests and interrogations undertaken by initiates of the ancient mystery schools. During the Crusades, knights and others from the West first came into contact with certain mysteries of the ancient initiatic schools in the East. In the ancient mystery initiations the candidates were asked questions. If they gave the correct answers, they were then eligible for certain recognition and acceptance. If they failed to answer correctly or had ulterior motives, then it was said they were subject to certain supernatural or karmic effects. The questions and the tests that the seekers of the Grail were subjected to, in the opinion of some scholars, bear a strong resemblance to the ancient initiatory rites, especially those having secrecy that was said to surround certain sacred knowledge.

There is another hypothesis with regard to the symbolism of the Grail. This is the idea that the Grail represented the quest for the *secret of life.* It too was reminiscent of the ancient secrets sought by both the physical and transcendental alchemists who desired to know the supreme secrets concerning the purpose behind life and the mystery of death.

The moral aspect of the quest for the Holy Grail is related to "the sacramental principles now accepted throughout Christendom and revered as the means whereby souls questing for life found life indeed. Consequently the Grail became the emblem of moral purity, or of triumphant faith, soldierly heroism, or gracious charity."

Godly hearts that,
grails of gold,
still the blood
Of faith so bold.

An allegory of the nature of the Grail is, of course, potential with mystical principles. Basically, the Grail conceived a person in purity searching for the power and wisdom that its sacred nature could reveal and bestow upon him or her. Those who lacked these moral virtues were to be frustrated and fail in their quest. Consequently, it is simple to substitute for the Grail the *Master Within.* By that term is meant a personal illumination, a spiritual awakening. the attaining of Cosmic Consciousness, or the mystical Oneness with the Absolute. Any of these terms would be mystically eligible as substitutes for the word Grail The quest, then, is for the pure in heart, the morally righteous person, who sets out to acquire the greater knowledge of self and its cosmic relationship.

The adventures experienced by Galahad in his quest for the Grail can likewise be interpreted as the human conflict with our own lower nature in trying to transcend it. If we desire to dramatise, or rather, to create an allegory depicting each person's individual search for the spiritual qualities of his or her own being and a channel within our own self which would lead to cosmic awareness, as well as the obstacles one would confront in this quest, then certainly the Holy Grail would be an excellent example.

Chapter 1

The Grail as a Miraculous Object

The Grail myth, which is about a knight's quest for a mysterious object has proved to be one of the most enduring myths of all time. Its strength as a dormant survivor in the human unconscious and its intermittent emergence into consciousness at various points in history may be attributed to two groups of factors. First, there is the human appeal of the quest, the challenges of the journey, the object itself, and its relative inaccessibility. And secondly, as in nature, there is the apparent cyclic nature of events in human society, in which elements of the Grail myth emerge into the consciousness of societies beset by intense crises (excessive and frequent violence, oppression, injustice, wars and civil strife, and today, impending environmental catastrophe), which represent the "lows" of the cycle of human "progress."

The age old Grail myth is a response, a counter balance to the "dark" side of events in history. It is an attempt to salvage something that has been lost or believed to have been lost in the human spirit, a new surge in the human soul to raise human consciousness to another "high" in the cycle, a triumph of ideals over harsh reality, a victory of self over ego or the liberation of the divine spark within humanity from subservience to desire. The myth takes hold when the need is felt to raise the consciousness of humanity to be proactive in creating or restoring a paradise on earth in order to counter the presumed inevitability of increased suffering caused by ignorance and error.

Seeking a mysterious object, a talisman or elixir, becomes important in this consciousness shift. It is the human acknowledgment of our inability to cope without aid, and our willingness to undertake a commitment to secure this aid. The object then becomes the goal sought out by the individual, that is, it drives and motivates the Journey because of its value. This value may lie in the selfish desire for power, but it later turns out to be something unselfish, noble, and inspirational to others; or else it is perceived to be what it is at the beginning and the end of the quest — a physical object or a symbol which provides the purpose for shaping the quester's destiny and, indirectly, the destiny of humanity.

Regardless of the origins of the earlier components of the Grail myth (be they Celtic, Middle Eastern, Asian, or of Medieval Christendom), its form as we know it took shape in the twelfth and early thirteenth centuries, commencing with the story of Perceval, or the *Legend of the Grail,* by Chrétien de Troyes. This was followed by several other accounts centred around the theme of the Grail quest. In Chrétien's poem, the Grail itself, which seemed to be a platter or dish, was carried into the refectory hall in a solemn procession during Perceval's visit to the otherworld castle of the Grail. Here, the Grail was described as being brighter than all the candles in the hall, consisting of pure, refined gold, and set with precious stones.

Magical Qualities

In various Grail romances, the Grail displayed other magical qualities: it "floated" into the room, it looked like a cup or stone, it temporarily blinded its beholders or made them speechless, it took the form of several images that appeared in a series before its beholders, it provided an inexhaustible à la carte menu to all the guests in the refectory hall, it maintained or extended individual lives, healed wounds, and restored fertility to barren land.

Shortly after Chrétien's poem was written, in which there was no suggestion as to the Grail being of Christian provenance, the Grail theme was soon Christianised (but not officially sanctioned by the established Church), by two other Grail writers, Robert de Boron and Heinrich von dem Thürlin. The former, in his poem *Joseph of Arimathea*, called the Grail the chalice of the Last Supper, which was also used to collect the blood of Christ at his crucifixion. The latter, in his *The Crown* described his Grail as a casket containing bread, which was accompanied by a blood - spotted cloth. The suggestion was obvious — a reference to the Eucharist was intended. There are many who see the Grail and its contents as a part of — or as symbolically explaining the meaning of the Eucharist. In this view, receiving communion once a week establishes contact between the seeker of the Grail (that is, the celebrant) and the Grail and its contents (that is, the active partaking of the body and blood of the Redeemer). This is the most popular view.

The Christianisation of the Grail was supported by another account which connects the Grail to Christ but not through the Blessed Sacrament. The romance called the *Grand St. Graal* asserted that the Grail. was a "book" written by Christ himself after the Resurrection; and yet another reference in the introduction to the *Lancelot Grail* mentions that a vision appeared before a hermit of the eighth century, during which Christ appeared to him and said: "Here begins the book of the Holy Grail, here begins the terror, here the marvels." This would make the Grail a record or storehouse of initiatic wisdom communicated to humanity by a great teacher in the priest-king tradition, represented by figures such as Melchisedek, Hermes Trismegistus, or Merlin, whether the book was written or communicated by word of mouth.

Initiatic Tradition

A most unusual description of the Grail. appeared in the romance of the anonymous writer of the *Perlesvaus,* or the *High History of the Grail.* Here the Grail was a shape-shifter. This, together with the Templar undertones of the romance as well as other references, suggest a strong connection with the initiatic tradition of the ancient mystery schools. Instead of the identity of the Grail being a single fixed object, it assumes a series of different forms before the awestruck beholder who sees images of a crowned and crucified king, a child, a man with a crown of thorns and wounds on his body, another indescribable manifestation, and finally, a chalice.

The transformations in this "movie" are accompanied by pleasant perfumes and an extraordinary brightness. The writer of the *Perlesvaus* seemed to be suggesting an initiation into some mystery cult, either Christian or another wisdom school. The images, and other references in the story, appeared to contain secret messages of a mystical nature, with deeper meanings, understood only by certain readers or listeners who look beyond the simple entertainment provided by the narrative.

However, it is the Grail, understood as a sacred cup and its sacred contents, the stories of its origins, its extensive journeys, the immense trouble taken by its protectors to conceal it from its enemies, and its transformative power on those who see or touch, it that has given the chalice the strong evocative content of today's myth.

The Glastonbury Cup

Over the centuries there seems to have arisen a national or regional pride in locating the Grail (whether a chalice or other object) in certain parts of Europe. The Glastonbury story associated with Joseph of Arimathea is matched by similar stories in France and Spain.

In England, the grail as chalice was popularised in the nineteenth century by Alfred Lord Tennyson, the poet, and in Germany by the composer Richard Wagner. In fact, not long after Tennyson wrote his *Idylls of the King,* it became known that a cup, a physical chalice made of olive wood, was in the possession of the Powell family, who looked after it for centuries at Nanteos, near Aberystwyth in Wales. It came into their possession shortly after Henry VIII broke with Rome and, implementing his policy of the dissolution of the monasteries, ransacked Glastonbury Abbey. Because of de Boron's legend of Joseph of Arimathea and its other Arthurian connections, Glastonbury was believed to be the resting place of the holy chalice.

Just before Henry's enforcers moved into the monastery, the story is told that seven of the chalice guardians (monks) escaped to their sister monastery at Strata Florida not far from Aberystwyth. Later, this monastery fell victim to the dissolution, but just before the intrusion, the seven monks (and their precious object) were given shelter at the house of the noble family of Nanteos, which was not far from the Abbey. Richard Wagner, twenty seven years before composing his opera *Parsifal,* actually visited the Powell family at Nanteos (1855), and reported that he had seen the olive cup. The Powell family moved to England and the cup has not been heard of since.

There are other stories about what happened to the Glastonbury cup. One relates that at the time of the dissolution of the monasteries, the cup was among the treasure that was split between two groups of monks who escaped to Wales. One group headed toward Strata Florida. The other followed the south coast of Wales and took shelter in the monastery at Caldy Island, taking the cup with them, where it still remains, of course, hidden forever!

A third version of the Glastonbury cup story is retold to us by Hank Harrison in his book *The Cauldron and the Grail.* According to this source, the trustees of the Chalice Well in Glastonbury have placed on the table of the attic at Chalice Well House their genuine Grail, along with the place settings at the table for the return of the twelve disciples of Jesus. Space prevents us from enumerating the several other secret Grail sites in the British Isles.

France and Spain

On the continent, the Joseph of Arimathea and Glastonbury story is matched by the visit of the Magdalene (Mary Magdalene) to Marseille in Southern France, and in Spain there is a Grail cup legend associated with St. Lawrence and the Huesca region.

As early as the fourth century the legends describe the Magdalene fleeing the Holy Land, taking with her something called the Grail. The story tells of this Grail being hidden in a cave in Southern France, cared for by the Cathars, a religious movement centred in the Pyrenees. In the early thirteenth century the Cathars were declared heretical and the Albigensian Crusade was launched against them. Just before the last stronghold of the Cathars, the fortress of Montségur, fell to the Crusaders and the surviving Cathars were burnt at the stake, about four or five of them escaped, taking with them some unknown treasure, which was believed to include the cup, and hid it in a cave somewhere nearby in the French Pyrenees. From there it was probably taken to the monastery of Montserrat near Barcelona.

The Spanish story traces the cup to St. Lawrence, a papal legate, who took the cup from Rome to a spot in the Huesca district in northeast Spain. It was hidden in a cave in the area where San Juan de la Peña monastery was built. Fear of impending Arab occupation led the cup's guardians to move it to the French Pyrenees, to Montségur or Montréal-de-Sos, or to both locations in turn, and then brought back to the San Juan de la Peña monastery. It was finally transferred to the cathedral in Valencia. It is probable that both stories refer to the same "Grail" associated with the Magdalene.

All this makes for fascinating reading, which is why the Rosicrucian Order, AMORC, has included in its extracurricular program a quest about the Grail Quest. Two Grail tours have already been completed by Rosicrucian students, offering the "pilgrims" first hand experience of sites, with appropriate commentaries, connected with all aspects of the history and mythology of the Grail and Arthurian legends. So far the "Grail Trail" has taken students to sites in England, Wales, Ireland, and Northern France. The final tour will cover Southern England, France and Spain.

The debates still continue as to whether the Grail is a physical object, an earthly talisman, magical and worthy of being revered as such, or a symbol of something in the human spirit which activates ameliorative change in individuals and societies. To a pilgrim's heart, its symbolic meaning is perhaps better understood if manifested in concrete form, a wisdom book, a magic cup, a precious stone, or a relic associated with a great religious teacher.

There are others who, in view of the speculative nature of the actual existence of the Grail object, prefer to express the Grail mystery in something less tangible but spiritually real, and in more meaningful terms. To some, says John Matthews, the Grail "Has no real existence at all, but [it] serves rather as a luminous idea that shapes itself at will to the needs of the individual..." And to others "it is part of an ongoing process of transformation, an alchemical dream of the soul on its quest for human evolution or oneness with God." The idea would seem to have sprung into the consciousness of being from various parts of the world at the same time or in different periods of human evolution, and given expression in the various myths of individual societies.

Geoffrey Ashe gives an added dimension to the Grail as a powerful idea, seeing it also as a special relationship between the Absolute and Humanity. He expresses this very warmly in his book, *King Arthur's Avalon:*

> *It [the Grail] was a visible pledge ... of God's friendship towards mankind ... [but] friendship can be tragically demanding and disruptive .... A knight who achieves, may wreck his life doing it. But the Grail rewards him with priceless assurance. God is there. God's hand reaches out through the cruelty and indifference of the world ... whatever the sacrifice, and that sacrifice is worth it.*

Chapter 2
The Stone that Fell from Heaven

The period of the full flowering of the Grail myth in literature occurred in the 12th and 13th centuries. During that time about a dozen romances on this theme were written by troubadours or court poets. The tales popularised the virtues of chivalry, courage, fairness, honour, respect for women, courtly love, and the protection of the weak. What made these poems different from other tales of adventure was the way in which the quest was linked to a mysterious object called the *Grail.* When the Grail myth was combined with the legend of Arthur and his Knights of the Round Table, the resulting fusion enhanced the power of the romances to set forth ideals of conduct intended to raise the consciousness above the ugly realities of life in the Middle Ages.

In the last chapter, "The Grail as an Object," attention was drawn to its identity as a physical object or relic, and also as a symbol of some spiritual goal or state of mind. As a physical object two ideas were touched on: the Celtic or pre-Christian Grail, which was a platter or container; and the Christian Grail, which related to the objects and purpose of the Eucharist. The source of these ideas derived from mythological elements of the "Matter of Britain and Ireland," embellished by the imaginative and creative skills of the trouvères and troubadours of France.

During the high period of the Grail sagas, a poet of the German school of Grail poets, Wolfram von Eschenbach, made a dramatic shift in the myth's content by giving it a more universal character. About twenty years after Chrétien de Troyes and Robert de Boron wrote their Grail romances, Wolfram wrote his *Parzival.* He claimed to have received his information about the Grail and its origins from a certain Kyot de Provence, who in turn obtained it from a document found in Toledo, Spain, that was written in Arabic. The presumed author of this document was a "heathen" astrologer called Flegetanis. The document stated that the Grail message was written in the stars and that, during the war in heaven between God's forces and the host of Lucifer, an emerald fell from Lucifer's crown. Standing aside from this great conflict were the "neutral" angels who, upon seeing the precious stone falling caught the emerald and carried it to earth, where they left it under the protection of the Grail family.

In this story the Grail was a *stone,* not a cup or some other object. Wolfram said it was kept in a castle named Montsalväsche (Mount of Salvation) and protected by Grail Knights, "a Christian progeny, bred to the pure life." The stone itself was thought to be endowed with marvellous powers, one of which was to impart immortality. There is some indication that mental alchemy played some part in Wolfram's thought. We note a reference to the idea that when the symbol of the stone is combined with that of the phoenix, it conveys dramatically the truths about life and death — an initiatory theme —with the stone acting as a catalyst so that the phoenix may rise from its ashes.

The name of the stone was *lapsit exillis*, and its spelling of what looks like two Latin words has caused much bewilderment as to its precise meaning. It has been called the "stone of exile," "stone catalyst," "fallen stone," or "stone of death." Perhaps Wolfram intended it to have a multiple meaning. Like the attributes of other forms of the Grail, this emerald was like a talisman in that it had the power to destroy, to nourish, to cause growth, to give and sustain life. This last power enabled the Guardians (who in Wolfram's poem were identified as Templars) to have a longer life or to look younger than their age.

The Grail and the Philosophers' Stone

Wolfram's Grail as a stone was, like some of his other ideas, a conceptual shift. In the earlier Welsh version of the Perceval story, entitled *Peredur*, the Grail Bearer in the Procession held a platter with a human head on it, blood and all. The French and other versions popularised the idea of the Grail as a *chalice.* Wolfram introduced this concept of the Grail as a *stone,* in the incipient stages of European alchemy, which became more widely known in the 14th to 17th centuries. It would seem as if the secret tradition kept alive through Grail literature was about to give way to another vehicle — that of transcendental alchemy.

In Wolfram's thought we can see the affinity of this stone with the mysterious stone of the philosophers. The Philosophers' Stone was said to transmute base metals into gold, lesser men into kings, or initiates into adepts, depending on whether one was talking about matter and its transmutation, or human beings and their transformation. Malcolm Godwin says on this point when assessing *Parzival*: "Many commentators have argued that the story of Parzival carries a hidden and secret astrological and alchemical description of how an individual is transformed from the gross body to even higher and higher forms"" (Godwin, p.170).

Wolfram actually encouraged his readers to "read between the lines" and consider his tales as initiatory documents. This is what many scholars have tried to do, by focusing their interest on such questions as these: Why did he state that Chrétien got the Grail story wrong by depending on the one source, a manuscript (now not known to exist) provided for him by his patron, Philip of Flanders? Why was Wolfram's source any more reliable? Why did he change the emphasis from the associations with the Christian mystery to something having Hermetic and Semitic overtones? Why did he bring in previously unheard of names like Kyot de Provence and Flegetanis? Why was the true story of the Grail found in a library in Toledo, Spain, where Jewish, Islamic, and Christian scholarship flourished and were enriched by the exchange of ideas in an atmosphere of tolerance? Why did Wolfram reflect alchemical and Rosicrucian ideas in his writings? Why did he equate the Knights Templar with the Grail Guardians? And, furthermore, why did he expand the Parzival story to include his father's adventures in Arabia?

Templar Knights and Knights of Islam

The scenario for the previous Grail and Arthurian romances was mainly Europe. Wolfram extended the setting to the *Outremer* — a medieval name for Palestine —where Christian knights were on the front line in the confrontation between Christianity and Islam. Yet, contacts were made at a higher level between the Knights Templar and the knightly orders of Islam. It became possible, through respect for the virtues of chivalry on both sides, for an exchange of goodwill and the opportunity to learn from one another. First-hand knowledge of the ancient mystery schools as they survived in the Outremer, together with Arabian science, alchemy, and Sufi mystical practices, were available to the Crusaders who were influenced by their contacts. It was to be expected that the Templars would incorporate some elements of ritual and initiatory practice into their own program of personal development.

Either Wolfram himself was a Templar, or he was closely associated with those Templars who had been exposed to the alchemical thought and initiatory rites of the mystery schools. It is therefore possible to assume that he used the Templars as the manifest model of the idealised conception of the Grail Guardians in his age. It is believed that they performed initiatory rituals in their commanderies that would place them in the spiritual lineage of the ancient mystery schools. They were a brotherhood effectively blending religious piety with exceptional military prowess in their outward activity, while practising rituals of a secret initiatic nature within their own circles so as to assist the spiritual advancement of their members. It has even been argued that the two persons mentioned in conjunction with the discovery of the Grail story — Kyot de Provence and Flegetanis — were not real persons, but were the respective pseudonyms for the two high Templar officers Hugo de Payens and Hugo de Champagne, and an Arabic book (the *Felek thanis)* of traditional secret teachings. In the light of Wolfram's avowed purpose of concealing names, places, and events in code, this idea does not seem too fanciful.

The notion of the Grail as a stone and the idea of making the Templars the Grail Guardians helped Wolfram to develop the main thrust of his message, namely, a fresh perspective of the Brotherhood of Man. His Grail sagas covered four generations of Perceval's lineage, and the scenario includes both Europe and the Orient. He attempted to show that dissimilar genetic inheritance, cultural variations, and religious differences can be accommodated at the individual and social level in the spirit of tolerance and love. We see this in the general plans of the stories.

Perceval and Firefiz

In his youth Perceval's father goes to Arabia and marries a Moslem queen. They have a son, Firefiz, who is thus the product of mixed cultures. Perceval is born of his father's second marriage to a woman of European race. The two, when they grow up, are professional knights who happen to engage each other in fierce combat, their identities being unknown. In the last stages of the skirmish they identify each other, put down their weapons, and embrace in brotherly love. The black and white Firefiz (note the alchemical colours) is finally given a place at the Round Table only reserved for Christians.

Most interesting is the way Wolfram uses the idea of the precious stone to develop a new concept of the Grail castle. His Grail Temple located at Montsalväsche "was seen as a microcosm of the universe topped by a huge ruby, representing the maternal heart of the world and called the Holy Rose. The whole imagery was absorbed, or most likely created, by the Rosicrucians" (Godwin, p. 160). But still more exciting is the effect on successive generations of his notions of the Grail Temple and its location. In most other accounts the Grail's home was an otherworldly castle (an image that describes psychologically the crossing of the threshold from the conscious to the unconscious). But in Wolfram's case, whether he intended to do so or not, the castle has been taken to mean an actual fortress in a specific place on earth. Places like the Cathar fortress of Montségur, or the monastery of Montserrat in the jagged mountains of the Pyrenees, or a cave in Languedoc, have become popular places of speculation and visitation.

Since the 1930s Montségur has been much worked over by excavation and written about by scholars and journalists. Its particular interest has been heightened by the fact that the fortress fell in 1244 to the Albigensian Crusaders, whose purpose was to eliminate the heretical Cathars, and also by the fact that this area of France was known to be frequented by Gnostics, Templars, alchemists, and Rosicrucians. Though not identical in their beliefs and practices, they all seemed to be part of the Great Tradition of esoteric wisdom dating back to Greece and the Fertile Crescent.

Wolfram, then, may be credited with enhancing the quality of the Grail myth, and it was to him that Richard Wagner turned as a starting point in the creation of his own operatic trilogy on the Grail sagas. The very idea of calling the Grail a (precious) stone, gives it a cross-cultural dimension in mythology. One could point to the emerald in the eye of Horus, the pearl on the brow of Siva, the stone in the castle of Brahma, which is like a small lotus flower. The jewel and its position on the forehead, for instance, is suggestive of the mystic Third Eye, the pineal gland, the organ of psychic perception or clairvoyance. The final Grail experience has been described as the equivalent of mystical illumination. It is also significant that, associated with religious or mystical figures of the past, we have read of the stone tablets of Moses, the Emerald Tablet of

Hermes, the Kaaba stone at Mecca (also fallen from heaven), the Lia Fail at Tara, and the Philosopher's Stone of the medieval alchemists, each having sacred or magical qualities.

Wolfram's stone, fallen from heaven, takes the Grail out of the Celtic "otherworld" and links it with the spiritual object of religious cultures across space and time. The world of the Grail in the Age of Chivalry, troubadours and Minnesänger, was, until Wolfram wrote his *Parzival* and the *Young Titurel*, European and Christian centred. This was a time when Christians and Moslems regarded each other as "infidels," militant competitors for the soul of humanity. Wolfram courageously brought them together in spirit amidst a climate of great intolerance of non-Christian doctrine, through his skilful use of allegory. By this early attempt to broaden the concept of the Grail, he challenges us in this world that technology has reduced to a global village, to bring to realisation the true quest of the Grail — that of spiritual development through personal effort linked with the need to transform humanity as a whole.

The author in front of the Diamond Stone, Avebury England

Chapter 3
The Grail Guardians

In the Grail romances of the 12th and 13th centuries, the Grail has been associated with a family who were its Guardians, and a special temple or castle, where the Grail was kept and protected by the Grail King and its Guardians.

The idea was given vogue with the appearance of Robert de Boron's Joseph *of Arimathea,* and the account entitled *Queste del Saint Graal* written anonymously. Both appeared within the last decades of the 12th century. Robert de Boron related that, after the Crucifixion, Joseph, the rich merchant who served Christ so devotedly and who collected the blood of Christ in the cup of the Last Supper, went on to establish a line of Grail Kings. They were expected to keep the secrets of the Grail (in this case, the chalice), and pass it down to their successors. They were Grail Kings by right of moral worthiness. In these and other Grail stories, in the context of Arthurian lore, the successors to the Grail King—that is, Perceval and Galahad — passed the initiation tests of Round Table Fellowship. Though all of Arthur's knights could be described as knights who sought the Grail, the literature places these two in the Grail King category. They were Knights of the Grail.

At the beginning of the 13th century, Wolfram von Eschenbach elaborated further on the importance of the Grail Guardians in his account of *Parzival.* He talks of Grail Knights who "who were bred to the pure life" and who had the special task of keeping the Grail. They were summoned to serve the Grail after they has passed a test of worthiness. Wolfram seemed to be suggesting that the hand of God, acting though the power of the Grail, or some other mysterious criteria, played some part in the recruitment. This in turn could imply that the Grail Knights were a closed, secret society, in which tests, ritual preparation, and initiatory rites were involved in the process of selection.

The Grail myth took shape in the time of the Crusades, when two religious faiths found themselves locked in holy war in Palestine for about 200 years. The Templars or Knights of the Temple, who played a leading part in the Crusades, seemed to manifestly play this role as Grail Guardians, as implied or stated in the accounts of three writers on the Grail myth. The anonymous author of the *Perlesvaus*, and Wolfram, in his *Parzival*, were chiefly responsible for identifying the Grail Knights with the Order of the Temple. Founded in AD 1118, the order started from a group of nine men, who took the sword to protect pilgrims in the Holy Land. It grew in size and influence over the next two centuries, acquiring fame for exceptional courage and fighting skill, and for high moral conduct. That the Templars also amassed great wealth through bequests of property, military success, and by acting as bankers, traders, and security agents in most of Europe and the Mediterranean, is also part of history. Mention has also been made of their influence in the building of the great cathedrals of Europe. Peter Bryce notes: "The Templars had the aim of guarding the routes to the Holy Land, which can be taken literally, but also in a more profound sense. Their activities put them into contact with other civilisations. They seem to have formed an intellectual link between East and West, and to have become Guardians of a Great deal of esoteric knowledge" (Bryce, p. 124).

Now, the author of the *Perlesvaus* betrayed, by the content of his story of Perceval, that he belonged to an Order of soldier-monks. This in itself would not be sufficient as an explanation for the author's anonymity, since the Church approved of militant Orders to defend the faith. But the writer went on to mention the presence of a conclave of "initiates" in the Grail castle, who were familiar with the Grail, and Perceval's meeting with "masters" who could summon 33 other knights by clapping their hands. The knights that appeared had Templar insignia and seemed "of an age". The mysterious or magical connotations implied here would not sit well with orthodoxy. Such references, however, and the writer's detailed knowledge of close combat and its effects on the human body, clearly pointed to Templars as the Grail Knights.

The Purest Knights

Wolfram was much less reticent to reveal he had some connection with the Templar Order. He was either a Teutonic Knight or Templar, and probably followed the Crusader track to the East. In his poem, he talks about the Grail being guarded by knights who are the purest, who seek adventure as a test of their worthiness, and who were also sent to be rulers of countries. If purity involved monkly asceticism, sacrifice of possessions, a willingness to die for a noble cause, and indomitable courage in the face of overwhelming odds, these attitudes found no better expression than in a Templar Knight. Wolfram actually coined a word for his Grail Knights; they were *Templeisen,* the iron men of the Temple. He also described the Grail King, whom they served, as one who ruled over an invisible brotherhood. This has Hermetic undertones — Grail Knights (Templars) were the physical embodiment of their archetype in Heaven.

That he meant to equate the Templars with the Grail Knights is confirmed in one of his later poems, the *Young Titurel.* The Grail castle here resembled a Templar fortress and even had a circular chapel, the way the Templars used to build them. He went on to say that the castle was guarded by Templar Knights. Such feelings about the Templars were shared also by other Grail writers. In the *Queste del Saint Graal* the sanctum or model of the home of the Grail resembled a model of the Holy Sepulchre, to be found in Templar commanderies everywhere, where the most sacred rites were performed. And Templar Knights guarding a magnificent "Temple" of the Grail is mentioned by Albrecht von Scarfenburg in his *The Younger Titurel (AD 1270).*

Some would argue that the Templar Brotherhood and the Guardians of the Grail were actually one brotherhood, not necessarily protecting a chalice or some other magical object. They could have been guarding something intangible, some secret, some "treasure," some special knowledge as a source of power, from which derived their moral strength and which made them superknights at that time, capable of transcending national and human boundaries. One of the implicits of the Joseph of Arimathea legend is that Jesus may have passed on some secret or secrets to Joseph, when the latter served his time in prison and Jesus visited him. This secret was to be passed on to the Grail keepers who succeeded him. If the Grail Guardians were conceptualised as a spiritual host, and if they were manifesting in some physical form on earth at a time when the Grail Legend enjoyed high popularity, then the Templars would be this visible example of service to the Grail.

The Templar Knights as Initiates

The intimate connection of the whole Grail myth with Templarism was zealously promoted in the first half of the 19th century. Intriguing articles appeared before the public which sustained the idea that certain baptismal fonts and vessels were like Grail vessels, that the Grail poems were written to glorify the Templar Order, that Templar symbols and doctrines were borrowed from the Grail Legend, that the same ideal of union of knighthood and sanctity was found in the Templar Order and the Grail Guardians, and so on (Waite, p. 562). It is even possible to envisage that the Templar Order (among others like the Teutonic Knights and the Hospitalers) was the manifest model upon whom the ideal conception of the Grail Guardian was built up by the Grail storytellers. This becomes especially significant if we place the Templars within the spiritual lineage of the secret initiatory tradition of the mystery schools. The Templars held their meetings in private, initiated their recruits within their chapels in secrecy, and defied external attempts by courts of the time, and by posterity, to discover the secrets in their "worship."

Common elements in thought and practice of certain initiatic schools which, due to their persistence over time and their value in raising the consciousness of humanity, have come to be recognised as representing that movement called the "Great Tradition." Its teachings were religious or mystical, usually not subject to the dogma of any particular faith. The Rosicrucian Order finds its roots in the mystery tradition of ancient Egypt. The inspiration and contents of this tradition have been reinforced through additions from the mystery teachings of individuals and groups in ancient Greece, China, India, Persia, and many other lands; not forgetting the contributions of modern science, philosophy. and psychology, and its own research which confirm or clarify the ancient wisdom of this tradition.

Historical links can be traced between the Rosicrucian Order, AMORC, and Rosicrucian activity in the late Middle Ages, that is, in the time of the Crusades, Templars, Alchemists, Cathars, Kabbalists, and Grail literature. The area of the most intense activity for all these groups was the south of France, although the movements were widespread throughout Europe. It is reasonable to assume that some Templars were Rosicrucians and vice versa, and the same could be said of Templars and Cathars, and Cathars and Rosicrucians. That some Templars fought in the Albigensian Crusade against Cathars does not negate the cross links between the movements, these Templars felt their first loyalty was to papal authority from whom they received their authority to function. On the Templar-Rosicrucian connection, not long after the suppression of the Templars as an Order, some Templars who survived or escaped the persecution formed a society called the

"Elder Brothers of the Rose-Croix" (Markale, p. 306).

Templar Grand Masters and advanced members of the Order would be categorised as higher initiates; they were distinct from other servants of the Order, like builders, artisans, men-at-arms, and ancillaries. The elevated station of their leaders had parallels with the Cathars, whose leaders were *perfecti,* perfect because of moral purity and strictly rule-bound. Others were *credentes,* believers, who were allowed some freedom from higher discipline and who were not yet ready to be elevated. Both Templars and Cathars derived some of their beliefs from contact with the Middle Eastern religious and mystical thought, which played no small part in their final condemnation as heretics and in the control of their overt activity.

Differences existed among the mystically minded societies. These are best seen in the main symbols representing their principal aim or character. The Templar Red Cross on a white mantle had a related but different symbolic meaning from the Rosy Cross of the Rosicrucians. A Cathar Cross was equal-branched with a rose at the axis. Rosicrucians as a group have never been known to go on military adventures, although individuals may have been combatants. Cathars defended themselves when attacked. The Templars' fame was partly based on their being a fighting machine. It also happened that Templar loyalty to papal authority saw some of them (perhaps unwillingly) take part in the Albigensian Crusade against the Cathars.

Rosicrucian and Templar Legacies

Yet all three movements were spiritually linked in that they emphasised personal responsibility for one's own spiritual progress, and inspired others by their exemplary conduct. And this is an important theme in the Grail Quest. The region of southern France, where Catharism flourished before the final suppression, and particularly the district of Toulouse, enjoyed for a while a freedom of thought and religion. Its people derived countless benefits from the activities of Templars, Cathars, and Rosicrucians. In England, too, there was some cooperation shortly after the Crusades between Templars and Rosicrucians: they built the Temple in London, which was to be used as a common ritualistic centre.

In general, these societies were applying and propagating in their own way their understanding about life and its meaning; they practiced initiatory models for the mystical advancement of their neophytes, and their rites relevant to this were conducted in strict privacy. Since Rosicrucianism is an eclectic, selectively inclusive, and progressive body of wisdom learning, it would have included the best of what the Templars thought and practised in their private and secret instruction. References to this interesting material is to be found in the archives of the Rosicrucian Order, AMORC, and the affinities between the two Orders are considered in the private instruction given to the Rosicrucian students.

Who were the Grail Guardians?

The question is sometimes asked: Is the existence of Grail Guardians mythical or are they historical figures? This leads to the same debate on the nature of the Grail — is it an object or symbol? There have been attempts to establish a lineage over the centuries — a succession of Grail Keepers — an actual rather than a legendary family, a physical bloodline that matched the spiritual one. A path is traced from the time of the Crusades, through the Merovingian dynasty, to Mary Magdalene and to Jesus. An apparent reference in Wolfram's work to an actual Merovingian ruler of a principality in the south of France is referenced for supporting evidence. With Wolfram's reputation as cryptic writer, the opinion is expressed: "The more one studies him, the more likely it seems that he is referring to an actual group of people, not a mythic or fictionalised family' (Baigent, p. 317). The evidence is a bit tenuous, and the conclusions either tend to raise a few eyebrows or thrill others with the connections explored. Corroboration by other research is wanting, but we must keep an open mind about this, as we take up another line of thought on the identity of the Grail Guardians. In this case the lineage is not genetic or fictional, but mystical.

In this view of the Grail King or Guardian we must turn to the Christian mystery. The name of *Melchisedek,* referred to in Hebrews 7:3, foreshadows Christ in his offering of bread and wine in token of the flesh and blood of his people. He appears to take on the character of a Grail King holding both offices of priest and temporal ruler, one who "is without father or mother or genealogy ... and continues a priest for ever." Jesus Christ is called "a priest in the succession of Melchisedek by right of sacrifice." There is no physical bloodline here, but an implication that the Grail King could only be a successor to the Melchisedek-Christ lineage, carried on as we have seen by Joseph of Arimathea into the future. The original chalice, or Grail, or its symbolic equivalent, and its protectors on Earth, were humanity's heritage from the time we acquired a religious or mystical consciousness.

This embodiment of the perfect Grail King does not sit well with some conceptions of the Grail romances about the Grail King. In the stories he appears as the ailing Fisher King, whose incurable wound was caused by some moral lapse. This lapse is explained as sexual indiscretion, or by the implication of original sin, or simply as illustrative of the Fall and the need for Redemption. Whatever the case may be, both King and Kingdom had to suffer indefinitely, or until some successor replaced the Old King. This is a problem we face when myths are mixed, and it occurred in the consciousness of medieval man when "pagan" beliefs (that is, Celtic) had to come to some accommodation with Christianity. We need not enter into the debate here as to whether the Biblical story is so much fact and so much myth. The mythical aspect of the Melchisedek succession supports a linear movement in human origins and destiny — from the Creation, the Fall, experience on Earth, and the final perfect outcome on Judgement Day. The Grail King myth, however, represents a cyclic Celtic view of events: what was observable in nature and the universe corresponded with events in the lives of people — birth, growth and decline, death, and regeneration.

Once the Melchisedek story and its implications entered into the consciousness of medieval people, it was represented, not in the Grail romance, but in stone. One of the countless messages that the cathedral of Chartres has passed on to posterity is the statue of Melchisedek. It stands alongside the Biblical and historical figures flanking the portals of the cathedral. He is there, holding a *cup* in which there is a smooth *stone,* as incorporating a double concept. The two symbols of chalice and precious stone, mentioned separately in the romances, are here united, as if to permanently set the myth in a medium even more enduring than oral or written tradition. Forever are the two truths represented — the chalice as a source and maintainer of life, and the precious stone as the light of cosmic wisdom.

And so we have found in the Melchisedek statue a point of meditation on the nature of humanity's place in the universe. The Grail Guardian here is the perfect man, the priest—king, the Christ-King, a composite of Arthur and Merlin, a Hermes Trismegistus, one who has attained office by being of two worlds, having one foot in Heaven and the other on Earth, or living this life in a moment of time as if the two worlds were one. This is surely the concept of the Grail Guardians in the imagery of Grail mythology, namely, to further the idea of Celestial Man. Every human being must be elevated through trial and initiation to the status of the priest-king, the union of the spiritual and temporal, the representation of divinity in the manifested universe in all its glory. The lineage of this elite may be marked out at the ideal or archetypal level, but no one is excluded from attaining this ideal since it requires individual will and effort in the first place, and then initiation into the highest degree of Grail chivalry.

A 19th Century Rosicrucian poster showing Leonardo on the right as "The Keeper of the Grail"

Chapter 4
The Home of the Grail

The subject of the Grail poses questions not only of what its nature is and who cares for it, but also *where* it is. Getting to know its hidden location and acquiring the competence or worthiness to gain access to it is an important challenge in the knightly quest.

According to some of the romances, the Grail's home was in a castle on a mountain difficult to scale, or on an island in the western sea, or in a lake hard to find, or in some cave, well, or temple, or other places that shielded the Grail from the eyes of the unworthy. Among these other places are a smiling valley, a paradise, a retired dwelling, a chapel, a feudal fortress, and finally, in Heaven. In many stories the castle, fortress or temple, is in a Waste Land, and the realm and home exist or seem to exist in another world, a fairyland. The myth tells us that those who are worthy shall find the Grail castle and Grail, whether they "lift their soul to God or open their soul that God may enter in." Those who are unworthy will never find it; the quest is not for them. It is also said that the quester has to be called, or chosen, and only finds the Grail by the grace of God, while others say that the Grail is no longer on Earth, having disappeared with Galahad into Heaven. This occurred on Galahad's last journey to Sarras, which some regard as being Jerusalem. One historian sees this visionary and earthly city as the model for the Grail Kingdom which, to the Crusaders, was a Paradise in the Holy Land. This image was helped by the fact that under the dome of the church there was a short marble pillar on which was placed a vessel containing a stone. So pilgrimage to the Holy Land was a quest for the Grail castle. (Sinclair, 17).

The Mount of Salvation

Great interest and excitement has been raised by writers about Grail literature on the location and character of the Grail's home as introduced in Wolfram's *Parzival.* Its popularisation was helped no less by the Grail operas of Richard Wagner. The Grail castle, he said, is on top of a mountain called *Montsalväsche,* Montsalvat, or the Mount of Salvation. He tells us also of the structure and significance of the Grail castle, and how the Templar Knights were its Guardians.

There is one place in the south of France that has excited extraordinary interest, which some believe to be the actual Montsalväsche, the Cathar fortress of *Montségur,* although it does not resemble the size and splendour of Wolfram's edifice. Known locally as the "Pog", it is in the French Pyrenees which in turn forms part of an area in France where a great intermingling of Christian, Judaic, and Islamic culture took place at the time of the Crusades.

Cathars as Grail Guardians

It is this region that was torn apart by the Albigensian Crusade against the Cathars and Montségur was one of their main strongholds. The Cathars, whose leaders were called *perfecti,* the perfected ones, strove to reach the highest form of spiritual life. In this respect, they resembled the Grail Knights. Their way of life was exemplary in that they were required to remain pure in body and mind. Catharistic elements entered into the events described by the Grail romances, events which compare closely with the *consolamentum* and *manisola* rites. Women could also be *perfecti,* Esclarmonde de Foix was one of their spiritual leaders. Even Wolfram's story about the emerald being brought to Earth by angles was a Cathar belief. Manichaeistic doctrine about the struggle between the forces of Light and the forces of Darkness, in which humanity was to be part of the struggle on the side of light in the cosmic drama, was also stated in Cathar terms. And the Grail of the troubadours always appeared in a blaze of light carried not by a priest but by a Grail Maiden. If Montségur was the home of the Grail, then the Grail was, or still lies, hidden in the area of the fortress. And if not, so we are told, it must have been smuggled out by the four Cathars who escaped before the fortress fell and then hidden in a cave somewhere in the Pyrenees.

Great interest was shown in the mystery of Montségur in this century from 1931 to the early forties, and intermittently after that. It was caused by a press article which stated that the Holy Grail was believed to be hidden in its ruins. A French authority on the subject (M. Arnaud), stated that the Grail and other treasures had been concealed somewhere in the underground vaults of the fortress, secure behind a massive concrete wall. An English antiquarian visited the scene and shortly after expressed the belief that something startling could follow the excavations that were being conducted. The digging went on for a while, but nothing startling was announced. About that time there were also books published by Otto Rahn, pointing to the 'fact' that Montségur was indeed Wolfram's Grail castle of Montsalväsche. In his *Crusade Against the Grail (1933),* he attempted to prove "that the Grail was a relic or a cult object of the Albigenses (Albi was a city in this Cathar region) and that information of a Catharistic nature was concealed behind the texts of the Grail poems, to avoid detection" (Jung & v.F., 15). In the last Chapter, mention was made that the Grail romances could have been written to justify the Templar Order. It seems now that the Grail Knights, Templars, and Cathars were being placed in the same alchemical vessel.

Be that as it may, Otto Rahn's searches attracted Nazi interest in the area. It is speculated that, during the Nazi occupation of France, the German excavations that were carried out at Montségur were intended to unearth the Cathar treasure or the Grail itself. But nothing was found that would help support the doctrine behind Himmler's Brotherhood of Grail Knights. Montségur has been able to conceal its secrets. It fulfilled the Grail castle's criteria of near inaccessibility. The fortress was built on wild rugged landscape, perched on a huge conical mass of limestone, with precipitous approaches on all sides; a good place to secure the Grail. If there was a Grail here, where did it come from? If it was the original Christian chalice, one would presume that it was the Grail that the Magdalene took with her to Marseille, and subsequently passed down through the centuries to the Guardians at Montségur. Its destination after it was smuggled from Montségur is unknown. One story makes its final destination as some cave in Sabarthez, not far from Montségur. Another tells of it being taken across the Spanish frontier into the Catalonian Pyrenees and finding safety in the monastery of *Montserrat.* The mountain range at Montserrat a few miles east of Barcelona, is very steep and jagged, difficult of access. Two things make Montserrat as impressive a site as Montségur. Local folklore makes a Jesus connection here. The jagged appearance of the mountains was supposed to have been caused by the earthquakes that shocked the Mediterranean world during the time of the Crucifixion. Furthermore, the alternative Medieval name given to the monastery of Montserrat was Montsalvat. The monastery would qualify as a temple, a sanctified place for a sacred object. Montségur was merely a fortress.

Grail Locations in Britain

There is support for the location of the Grail castles on mountains in other parts of Europe. Wales has two places, one on the southwest coast, and one in the north. A sharp hill rises up behind the township of Llangollen, and supports a few ruins of a castle that once stood there, named *Castell Dinas Bran.* Nearby flows the river Dee. Legend has it that the castle was the home of the Welsh king Bran, who was also regarded as the Fisher King. The name points to its origin in the Celtic god, Bran, who possessed a Cauldron of Plenty, capable of feeding 500 people, cowards excepted. Bran was also the Welsh god of the sea, and the sea and fishing go together. In the waters of the river Dee, we could imagine the Fisher King fishing. Again, the Welsh Peredur and Chrétien's Perceval, the same hero in the two versions of the myth, was brought up in the forested mountains of Snowdonia in North Wales. The Welsh Grail castle at Llangollen is on the east side of this range. Moreover, Bran, like the Fisher King, had wounds that would not heal. And finally, it seems more than coincidence that Bron (with a name similar to that of Bran), the relative of Joseph of Arimathea, was also the Grail Guardian to bear the designation of "King Bron". A recent Rosicrucian Grail Tour explored relevant Grail and Arthurian sites in the area of North Wales. The visitors noted its strong Arthurian connections. Among these were the district named after Gwalchmai (Gawain), the ruins of Dinas Emrys (Merlin's castle abandoned by Vortigern), Lake Llydaw (home of the Lady of the Lake), the Pass of the Arrows (site near Arthur's last battle). All these point strongly to the Celtic contribution to the Grail myth and explain their attachment to Castell Dinas Bran as being the home of the Grail.

But if we descend from these high and remote places, we can hear reports of other sanctuaries for the Grail on somewhat lower ground, yet no less mysterious for their ability to keep the Grail hidden from unworthy human eyes. For instance, the Scots have their claim to keepership, if not guardianship, of the Grail's home. The Grail they say, is in the *Rosslyn Chapel*, Edinburgh, and lies hidden somewhere in its white, sculptured stone. Now, Rosslyn Chapel is a treasurehouse of Templar and Masonic symbolism. For many years legend had it that the Grail cup was buried under the 'apprentice column' of the chapel. The column looks similar to one of two columns mentioned in Freemasonic ritual. A descendant of the family who owned the site had some excavations conducted at the chapel in which earthscan equipment was used before digging. One hoped in this way to locate and eventually to retrieve the cup.

However, the scans did not reveal the presence of the cup in the column or in the walls. But at some part of the floor, it looked as if a cup was buried underneath. Sure enough, the excavation that followed brought out a cup, but it was identified as a receptacle used by a seventeenth century mason to hold his lunch! (Sinclair, 86—7). This, however, has not subdued the enthusiasm of the true believers who continue to assure others that the Grail is still there. And they may be right, if the symbol for the Grail is altered to mean that it is a secret message coded in the symbolism of this unusual chapel.

Further south, in England, the work of Christian clerics, Arthurian legend, and the Joseph of Arimathea story, have made *Glastonbury* more popular as the Home of the Grail. It is acknowledged as the mystic *Avalon,* and the Grail's resting place, no matter where it may have been or travelled before. Avalon, in Arthurian legend, is the otherworldly island in the west, where Arthur's sword was forged and to which Arthur, after receiving his fatal wound at Camlann, was taken away by three queens to be healed. In the Celtic tongue, Avalon suggests a land of apples. A report of Gerald of Wales (1170 AD) confirmed the finding of a Cross, with Arthur's name on it, in a grave supposed to contain the remains of Arthur and Guinevere, in the churchyard at Glastonbury. Another account by a contemporary referred to the burial of Arthur in the island of Avalon. This contrasts with the legend that Arthur was not buried at all but kept in a cave, waiting to return to England at her time of need. But despite the doubts about the exhumation of Arthur's body at Glastonbury, the site in the Abbey draws thousands of pilgrims every year!

In past times, Glastonbury's plain flooded in winter and became a shimmering, foggy fenland, also known as *Ynis Witrin,* the Isle of Glass. It was only accessible in summer on foot. Glastonbury is the home of the mystic *Tor*, with its strange spiral peregrinations around its conical rise and talk of its many underground tunnels. The Chalice Well near its base has healing waters. Some stories suggest that the holy chalice, be it Grail or not, is hidden in its depths. A shoot from the staff of Joseph of Arimathea, which became the thorn tree at Wearyall Hill, still grows (that is, a scion from successive trees) on the cathedral grounds. So all this, plus talk of ley lines passing through Glastonbury, and the fame of the monastery that once stood there as an important spiritual centre from Arthur's time to Henry VIII, made it a sacred site with Grail associations. Glastonbury has not a Grail castle or temple. But the whole district must be seen as a natural complex which, by topography, geomantic connection, and human activity, has made it a so-called entry point to the Otherworld realm of the Grail. Travellers today, when driving through the district of "Avalon", may get the feeling of being absorbed from a material world into an ethereal one. One has to explain this mood or feeling in terms of a "mental set" conditioned by romantic literature or find an explanation in metaphysical or mystical terms.

The Oriental Hypothesis

Most intriguing is the description of the Grail castle or temple by a German poet, Albrecht von Scarfenburg, in his *Younger Titurel* (1270 AD). He places the Grail Home on a mountain of Onyx stone, and describes in detail its appearance and construction. We would expect the writer of the romance to be rich in imagination when he described the wondrous palace fit to house the remarkable object. However, his imagination must have played only a small part in this. Either he showed a high degree of clairvoyance, or he had obtained a description of the temple from an actual temple elsewhere. There is also the possibility that the temple was constellated in his unconscious mind in resonance with a similar mental construct of the original builders of an actual temple that once existed in early seventh century Persia, called the "Throne of Arches". This temple was "a mandala shaped structure, representing paradise, or a spiritual world beyond whose prototype" may be seen "in the Parsee sanctuary of the Holy Fire at Shiz" (Jung & v.F., 107). The region where Shiz lies has an unusual atmosphere. It seems to focus the most beautiful light on earth, softens the hardness of the landscape, and gives the appearance of making the mountains levitate. The heat, the quality of light, and dryness, seem to deaden the senses and open up another sort of perception, a mystical one. In this place was built the Throne of Arches. Archaeological evidence and reports of contemporary sources showed a striking resemblance of the actual structure with Albrecht's visualisation. "It was domed, roofed with gold, and lined with bluestones to represent the sky. There were the stars, sun and moon, astronomical and astrological charts outlined in jewels, balustrades covered in gold, golden staircases and rich hangings". (Matthews, 1.23) Albrecht had described his temple as resting on a mountain of onyx which was kept polished at the top, and it had a lake beside it. The actual temple was built on a crater, whose mouth had become a lake. The mineral content of the waters had turned the shores dark enough to look like onyx. All this lends support to the theory, along with other historical records, that the Grail myth could be of oriental provenance. But that is one side of the story.

Megalithic Star Temples

We must go back to the far west of Europe to find an earlier prototype of the Grail temple. The mystical concept of the Grail temple may go back to the period of the Megalithic builders (6000 — 2000 BC). It was the time of the building of Stonehenge, Avebury, Newgrange and others, described variously as passage graves, observatories, and star temples. In these and other stone monuments the basic symbols of earth (the square), and the heavens (the circle) were combined to represent the coming together at appropriate times of the sky god and the earth goddess. People involved themselves at these numinous moments with their sacred rites. The spots chosen to build these structures were not haphazard. These early Neolithic people were sufficiently advanced in sacred geometry, mathematics, astronomy, and geomancy, to be able to find places on the earth's surface where earth's energies were strongly focussed. Its purpose was to attract the energies of heavenly bodies. Newgrange provides us with the most dramatic example of this three-way sacred contact between sky, earth, and humans. At mid-winter sunrise a shaft of light comes through the window-box of a long passage into the huge mound or star temple. It slowly lights up very tenderly the long, pitch-dark passage and moves into the large corbel-roofed central chamber. Once there, its brightness is increased by the reflection of quartz crystals in the walls. The central ritualistic object is a stone carved in the shape of a font or large cup, which obviously had some sacred contents that figured in the ritual associated with this annual event. Need we spell it out? This could have been the proto-Grail! The central chamber could accommodate 30 people at a pinch — as the Rosicrucian party on the last Grail Tour found out when they meditated together in total darkness and lost themselves in the wonder of that mystic moment. It was after this visit that one could truly understand the depth of thought and feeling that went into the construction of magnificent temples of any sort. One shares with John Matthews his thoughts on the Grail Temple. "In its most complex and complete form," he says, "the temple was a cosmic mirror, which becomes an initiator into the divine mystery of creation, the most perfect object of the Quest (meaning the soul's spiritual quest) ... it conforms to the traditional archetype". (II.73).

What is the Grail Castle?

We may now ask, how does the Grail Knight fit into all this? We know that the hero of the Grail romance tries to find that Kingdom of the Grail, whose castle or temple is where the Grail resides. All his adventures on the journey are a projection of an inward spiritual journey. The "Home" may be a mansion of the soul where the Grail of transformation is to be found. If we see ourselves as the Grail Knight, we may each see ourselves as the temple (ourselves as we should be), and the Grail as a jewel in this temple. "In the centre of the castle of Brahma, our own body, there is a small stone ... and within can be found a small space. We should find who dwells there and want to know him... for the whole universe is in him and he dwells within our hearts" (Quoted by Matthews, (2) 84, from the *Chandhogya Upanishad)*. In like manner the fifteenth century mystic, Teresa of Avila, calls upon us to centre our lives, by using the castle image *(The Interior Castle)*. The soul must journey from the outer environs of the castle, facing all sorts of demons before reaching the seventh, which is the inner core. The journey is harrowing at times, full of despairing moments, but the end is rewarding. The seventh chamber is where the gem is found, where the human soul melts within the Divine or Universal Soul.

Such descriptions of the Grail Castle and Grail Kingdom reveal to us, through our imagination and a shift in consciousness, how the invisible "Otherworld" (the world which we find so hard to perceive), and the visible, tangible world, which we understand as reality — can somehow in the Quest merge into one, and this even suddenly and unexpectedly. This moment of "inner" perception happens in meditation, in dreams, or when gazing with concentration on some white surface or a still pool, and in the emotionally uplifting moments we sometimes experience. This is a truth that was infused into the Grail romances. We are all on the frontiers of two worlds, once we set out on the quest. Some cross over sooner than others, from the lesser to the higher, and then return to tell the tale. Others stay on the frontier and fail to step across. So we are taught by the examples of Galahad, Perceval, Bors, Gawain, Lancelot and the other knights. Each of the Knights of the Round Table was a temple of one sort or another, hidden within each was the Grail. Galahad and Perceval succeeded, the one ascended to Heaven, the other became the Grail King. Bors, having seen the Grail, returned to tell the story. Gawain and Lancelot, despite their great virtues, failed to make the sacrifices required of them. While the Grail romances can inform us about the path to the Home of the Grail, it is just possible that they may also inspire us to take up the challenge to tread the same ground of adventure, uncertainty, despair, hope, excitement, and wonder, to reach the Kingdom of the Grail.

A picture by Camden in 1607 of the lead cross found on a grave supposed to contain the remains of Arthur and Guinevere, in the churchyard at Glastonbury. The translated inscription reads; 'Here lies buried the renowned King Arthur in the Isle of Avalon'.

Chapter 5
Mysteries and the Grail

For several centuries before the first written accounts of the Grail legend appeared, Europe experienced a dark age of turmoil and despair. Living conditions throughout Europe were poor and the spiritual life of the people was at a low ebb. Feudal Europe was divided into dozens of competing fiefdoms and feudal states. There were no national political entities. For example, the same lord might hold lands in both France and the Holy Roman Empire. Smaller kingdoms and principalities were constantly at war with one another and territorial boundaries were redrawn at a terrible cost in human life and suffering. Violence, insecurity, misery, and intolerance marked the state of society.

The only central authority covering a wide area, in a spiritual sense, was the Church of Rome. But its ability to temper civil and political excesses was limited due to a number of factors. In launching the Crusades against Islam, the Roman Church saw an opportunity to turn the energies of warring political units in Europe against a common foe.

Following Mohamed's death in 632 Islam expanded rapidly. In the East, the Holy Land was conquered in the seventh century and Moslems penetrated outposts of the aging Byzantine Empire. Toward the West, Islam spread rapidly across North Africa, and by the eighth century, had conquered much of Spain. From Spain, Moslem armies poured across the Pyrenees into France. Initially repelled by the Franks and later Charlemagne, the Moslems eventually reconquered much of Spain. In the ninth century the Balearic Islands, Sardinia, Corsica, and Sicily came under Moslem control, and they repeatedly invaded Italy, plundering Rome and besieging the Pope in his own fortress.

By the eleventh century Christian Europe, although still divided, was strong enough to begin a counter offensive. Kings of Leon, Castile, Aragon, and Navarre, aided by French knights, recaptured almost half of Moslem Spain. French knights founded the kingdom of Portugal. The Moslems were driven out of Corsica. And a Norman adventurer, Roger de Hauteville, conquered Sicily by 1091. The First Crusade to recover the Holy Land began in 1096.

The Crusaders

In these wars of one faith against another, it was expected that the spiritual kingdom of God on earth would be further strengthened by enlisting the combined might of temporal power on its side. The unifying symbol was the Holy City of Jerusalem — holy in fact to three contending faiths. But the objective was to ensure that Jerusalem would be kept within the Christian fold.

Form the 11th to the 13th centuries, the Crusades, aside from their excesses, did much to achieve some pan-European solidarity, reduce internecine conflict, and increase religious fervour. A renewal of the human spirit and a new period of intense activity in religious thought and political life began to manifest, as evidenced in art and architecture, in literature and scholarship, and in movements that presented a challenge to church doctrine.

At the mystical level, centres of Gnostic, Hermetic, and Kabbalistic thought dotted the landscape. To a great extent, contact with Islam — a result of the thrust of Arab expansion towards Europe — was instrumental in bringing about these developments. During the Crusades, Christian knights were on the front line in the conflict between Christianity and Islam. However, contacts were also made at a higher level between the Knights Templar and the knightly orders of Islam. First-hand knowledge of the ancient mystery schools as they survived in Palestine, together with Arabian science, alchemy, and Sufi mystical practices, was available to Crusaders who were influenced by their contacts. The most important result of Crusader contact with the Arabs in Palestine, and with Islamic states in Western Europe was the opening up of a track of communication between two opposing religious cultures. Both were unyielding in doctrine. But at the mystical level, the separation of the three monotheistic faiths — Islam, Judaism and Christianity — all having a common source, were coming close to each other again.

A Rich Blend of Cultures

During the Middle Ages Spain was a meeting point of the three religions and three world views. Christian, Moslem, and Jew were able to live there under tolerant rulers, and scholarship of a cosmopolitan character flourished. This attitude spread gradually to other parts of Europe. Troyes, in France, was one of these centres, where Chrétien de Troyes wrote his Lancelot and Perceval romances, giving emphasis to ideals of chivalry, courtly love, and individual initiative. Troyes was also a centre of Kabbalistic thought, a place where the "white monks" or Cistercians were established and whose leader, St. Bernard, had made it possible for the Templar movement to be established under the authority of the Church.

Languedoc and Provence in Southern France were regions where "new age" movements seemed to be replacing Rome as a centre of spiritual influence. This was the land of the Cathars, Rosicrucians, Kabbalists, the Black Virgin cult, Gnostics, and of European and Sufi mysticism. The troubadours, who came out of this region, carried some of the region's "heretical" ideas all over Europe. In Spain, Toledo and nearby cities had impressive libraries, where many Classical, Sufi, and Hebrew texts were to be found. According to Wolfram von Eschenbach, who wrote the Hermetic version of Parzival, the source of his work was a document found in Toledo, written in "heathen" script. In many of Toledo's public buildings, churches, and cathedrals, one sees evidence of a successful blend of Christian and Moslem styles in art and architecture. The tolerance of both Christian and Moslem cultures in Spain can be clearly seen in a Templar Church in Segovia, not far from Toledo, which displays a painting of a Moslem at prayer.

This changing scene in Europe constituted a serious challenge to the Church, which had strengthened its position at the end of the millennium as the recognised head of Christendom. Now new challenges, new "heresies," were causing much discord: there were Cathars with their Manichean doctrine, Templars who were allegedly practicing heathen rites, the feminine thrust of Gnosticism associated with the Magdalene cult, the Alchemists and their mysterious practices, and Grail Christianity or mysticism being spread by the troubadours and poets in the courts throughout Europe.

In defensive response to these movements the Church took several steps, among which, it raised or encouraged Mary's status as an object of adoration, and it occasionally eliminated individual Alchemists — claiming they were sorcerers. However, the Grail poets were neither officially condoned nor condemned because of their skill in walking the razor's edge between orthodoxy and heresy. This may be noted in the group of Grail literature called the *Vulgate*

Cycle, the work of Cistercian monks, who worked both Catharistic and Orthodox themes into the content of the romances.

We have previously called attention to the anonymously written *Perlesvaus* and Wolfram's *Parzival.* Both these works contained Christian, as well as unorthodox and pagan elements. Celtic and Oriental references, aspects of astrology, Gnosticism, Hermeticism, and secret initiatic sequences are skilfully woven into the narratives.

New Spirit in Religion and Philosophy

The essence of this new spirit in religion and philosophy is well stated in Malcolm Godwin's comment on the Perceval story. "Perceval," he says, "embodies the search of medieval man for some higher knowledge which would give some significance and meaning to life, which the Church was unable to offer". (Godwin, p. 176). It may be described as a kind of Grail Christianity which focused on esoteric mysteries, as against Church teaching in which the exoteric form mattered more. The two greatest threats from within the Church were settled to its advantage when in 1244 and 1308 respectively the Cathars and Templars were annihilated as overt and organised groups — in both cases this was done by force of arms and papal authority. Their ideas and practices, however, persisted in other forms and places, in secrecy, as if by some historical necessity or inevitability.

What is described as a secret initiatory tradition, modelled on the ancient mystery schools, survived in Europe in various forms, as had such traditions in the past during times of intolerance and persecution. The view being presented in this chapter is the view of some writers in the area of esoteric studies: that the Grail myth was a projection into literature of this secret tradition. Had the Grail myth been reconstituted from earlier folklore or tribal myths, the Grail myths may have simply become part of a general collection of local mythology. They became more important however because they had a double intent in their reconstituted forms, and were read or heard across Europe.

The underlying philosophy behind the heroic tales of the Grail knights was a declaration in favour of an alternative to the life specified in Church teachings. This alternative lifestyle advocated personal responsibility in the shaping of one's life, through the application of effort and endeavour, and the use of free will. To achieve humanity's divine purpose, the individual was to be the initiator of his or her own destiny, not merely the passive recipient of the grace of God to be received as a gift or earned by faith and prayer. As one writer puts it: "The Knights of the Round Table went in quest of the Holy Grail ... they undertook a commitment, they did not stay in Camelot and pray that the Grail would come to them" (Knight, p. 163). Clearly, the Grail writers were presenting a different view of "salvation" and how it was to be achieved.

Galahad, the Hero-Knight

The Perceval story points the listener or reader towards an understanding of life, of certain mystical truths relating to birth, death, and regeneration. Just as Christ was a model for all Christians, so Perceval represented the finest example of medieval man. With greater Christianisation of the myth, Perceval was replaced by Galahad to make the hero a more Christ-like figure. In any of these versions, however, their effect on people at that time must have been considerable. The stories possessed a secret transformative power. One could imagine the troubadour and minnesinger playing the part of the initiatory "master," taking the "neophyte" (the reader or listener) through the joys and ordeals of the journey. The initiate is charged spiritually. He or she may feel at the end of the journey "twice-born" and become aware that they are in possession of certain secrets.

Such conclusions have been reached by a number of writers who have pursued research into the Grail myth. It was G. A. Heinrich (*Parzival and Wolfram von Eschenbach)* who first noted that what Perceval experienced was less of a series of adventures than a series of initiations. Jessie Weston explored the idea of the myth being a reenactment of ancient vegetation rites. And it was W. H. Nitze who stated that the more advanced readers of the romances "could identify a hyper-text by secret words or gestures learned only through initiation" (Harrison, p. 93).

More recently, Trevor Ravenscroft points to the symbols appearing in the Perceval story as a clue revealing the method of the traditional initiatory schools, namely, the passage of the initiate through seven degrees of progress towards enlightenment. It is to be noted that, in making this comparison, the symbols in the Grail Quest are not identical with but similar to those of the ancient mystery schools. They represent broadly the experiences of the initiate as he or she proceeds from the state of foolish innocence to that of the fullness of mystical understanding. Some degrees are represented by birds — the raven, peacock, pelican, phoenix, and eagle — to indicate the inner Journey into the unconscious, the messages received from it, the workings of the imagination, the refinement of the initiate's feelings, the exploration of the inner world and reactions to it, and the expansion of his or her consciousness through space. The older degree of "warrior" or "soldier" is replaced by the "knight"; this is the Grail knight who brings justice to the world by the use of a discriminating sword. Where a degree used to be the "Persian" or "Egyptian", we have a nameless Perceval at sometime during his life receiving his name in an intuitive flash; he becomes an identity through the "conversion of suffering". The lion encountered by Gawain, Perceval's alter ego, symbolises the acquisition of conscious control over his unconscious prejudices. The highest degree was the Crown or Grail Kingship.

As a final comment it would be of interest to look at the intentions (as far as we can interpret them) and ideas presented in the Grail romances of two of the most important writers, namely, Chrétien de Troyes (*Legend of the Grail,* c.1180) and Wolfram von Eschenbach (*Parzival* c. 1210). Both Chrétien and Wolfram were, speaking figuratively, masters of instruction by way of the romantic drama. Both were communicating some "secrets" of the mysteries relating to the purpose and destiny of humanity, the correspondence of life with the cycles of nature, and the message of return to primordial man. The approach of the soul towards the Grail, in Chrétien's poem, was represented as an individual quest. The individual struggles towards wholeness (to use the language of depth psychology), that is, towards the Grail. The struggle was necessary to heal the splits in the individual's psyche in order to achieve self-realisation or spiritual health. It was the same with Wolfram's hero — the splits could be identified as those between nature and "supernature," between Earth and Heaven, between illusion and reality. The Grail was the point of reconciliation or merging of these opposites.

Wolfram was no less concerned with the individual than was Chrétien, but he broadened his horizon. This was in keeping with this more emphatic esoteric orientation. He wanted to save the human race, and saw the individual as participating in some cosmic purpose. And incidentally, this was in harmony with the teaching of the Church, which discourage the individual and unmediated search for salvation. But to Wolfram, the closed system of one faith was not enough. The Grail Quest was for humanity as a whole, starting with a reconciliation of the three antagonistic faiths — a reconciliation that transcended, at the mystical level, doctrinal differences. In essence this was the way of the Alchemist, the Kabbalist, and the ancient initiatory orders.

One must also clear up a misunderstanding here. Wolfram's idea that the Grail Guardians were "bred to the pure life" and his tendency to emphasise the importance of the ancestral (that is, the family lineage) factor has been misconstrued by some. The most nefarious distortion occurred after Richard Wagner's presentation of Wolfram's message in his operatic trilogy based on the Grail sagas. When Adolph Hitler came to power, he twisted the theme of spiritual leadership to suit his own racial superiority theories. As we know, the consequences were disastrous. A truer understanding of Wolfram's esotericism identifies the Grail Guardians as the most advanced, mystically developed group, coming from all lands and cultures, bred in the initiatic tradition, and representing the vanguard of humanity's progressive evolvement on the mystic path.

It is this mystical aspect that was the "mystery" that Wagner attempted to present in his Grail operas, and he succeeded. The visual perception of the individual's quest to their "centre," magnificently dramatised, with all the strength of the music medium, pointed to the Biblical story of the fall and redemption of humanity. In terms of the core of any religion, Perceval's story represents humanity on a return track to its own divinity. Psychologically, it demonstrates to us all the "process of the inward way of reintegration, the engrafting of the new self upon the old" (Wilmshurst, p. 6). In mystical terms, "both the true hero and the mystic have to die to their egos, die to the idea of who they are, in order to be reborn as something else or something greater." (Godwin, p. 228).

The theme of this chapter, the Grail in Mystery, may be seen as an application of the symbolic power of the Grail to transform individuals and humanity as a whole. Its greatest mystery is that it has such a hold on our psyche. We reach out and we reach within in order to understand the Grail's secret; if we come to know it, such knowledge is beyond compare. It may be less mysterious when, through striving, we come to know that we are participating in the mystery, and in so doing derive the utmost satisfaction from being aware of our contribution to a vast energy force shaping the universe. Such knowledge must give one the power to attract all of humanity to search for order and meaning in the complexity of life in this world.

1583 Woodcut: The Universe Arising From the Grail
(*From a MS in the Metropolitan Museum of Art*)

Chapter 6
The Grail in Alchemy

The last chapter on *The Grail in Mystery* explored the theme of the Grail myth as a didactic part of the mystery tradition. By and large, the Grail poets wrote their works for entertainment, the fruit of their genius was open to all, but their real message was veiled in mystery. Yet it was less mysterious to those who were discerning. The disseminators of the mystery were the troubadours who took the tales to many a court.

The period of maximum literary output in Grail literature (c. 1170—1210) gave its last flicker with the story of *The Younger Titurel* (1270), by Albrecht von Scharfenberg. And only three significant primary works entered the historical landscape after the 13th century. These were the poems of Thomas Malory *(Morte d'Arthur,* 1485) and Alfred Tennyson *(Idylls of the King* 1856—74); the third were the mystical operas of Richard Wagner, composed in the late 19th century.

Wolfram von Eschenbach as Grail Alchemist

Though the high period of Grail literature passed by, contact was not lost between Grail mysticism, which characterised the literature, and its deeper background and source, the secret mystery tradition. The Grail movement simply yielded place to the alchemist. The straddle over the two forms of mystical or spiritual expression occurred with the work of the hermetic genius, Wolfram von Eschenbach who, in his *Parzival* reconstituted the Grail myth with a successful blend of European and Oriental mysticism and alchemy.

Alchemy, as popularly understood, was intent on the chemical transmutation of metals into finer stuff — the 'purest' metal being gold. To some within the alchemical movement however, the interest in the search for gold by chemical processes was possibly a subterfuge which concealed the work of the transcendental alchemist. The latter was concerned with spiritual change within themselves and humanity in general, and may be described as an early form of practical psychology and mystical philosophy; it was a world view and a form of action aimed at changing human nature (or transforming it), without recourse to guidance from any religious doctrine or Church mediation. Others see this face of alchemy as an attempt to apply in matter those principles that worked to effect spiritual change in humanity, in other words. it was not a pretext for something else, but an attempt to apply the hermetic law of correspondences, "as above, so below."

Exploring the nature of alchemy as it manifested in the 15th to the 17th centuries, one cannot help but recognise the affinity between the objective of this art/science and the transformative values of the Grail Quest. The alchemist's workshop was the place where things were to happen, just as the forest and the 'otherworld' were the field of experience for the Grail knight. Both alchemy and Grail mythology had their metaphors for the total psyche, its dynamic, and its direction for optimum psychic health. The vessels that symbolise the Grail, as they appeared in different accounts of the romances and in the alchemist's workshop, were associated with the initiatory process: platter, cup or chalice, casket or stone were analogous to the crucible, flask or alembic. The content in either case was a transforming substance or substances to which was added the fire of experience and the stone of wisdom, the necessary parts of the initiate's consciousness-raising program. McLean notes that each form of the Grail knight's quest could be seen to play a significant role in the elevation of humanity: the platter provided spiritual nourishment, the chalice offered redemption or grace, and the stone brought about enlightenment, and "these alchemical processes taking place in the vessels were tinged with Grail esotericism". (p.64).

Cathedrals Communicate the Secret Tradition

The overlap of Grail symbolism and alchemy, together with elements of astrology, the Kabbalah, and ancient mythology, found a comfortable mix with orthodox Christianity in the famous Gothic Cathedrals of Notre Dame. Their sculptured art, architecture, and stained-glass windows have left a lasting record of medieval people's attempt to unify their total experience. On the Grail theme we may draw attention to the relevant images in Chartres Cathedral. The statue of Melchisedek, placed among numerous statues on the portals, shows him bearing the Christian Grail cup with the hermetic stone of Wolfram placed in it. Both Grail symbols were combined and linked with the theme of the priest-king, a ruler whose spiritual and temporal dominions are one. A window shows the "joust in Heaven" between a Christian and a Saracen knight, meant to represent Perceval and Firefiz, his half-Saracen stepbrother. The lance of one is fractured in the middle, and the other is held straight on impact, so that between the two knights a triangle is formed reminding one of a law symbolised by that geometrical figure. The skirmish seems to be taking place in some space between earth and sky. In the story the two brothers, recognising each other later, embrace each other. The whole symbol shows the reconciliation of contradictions at a higher spiritual level. There is also, on a "portal of initiation", a statue of the Ark of the Covenant (some would say, another form of the Grail) brought by an ox-cart from Jerusalem to Chartres. Such specific references to the Grail myth form part of a veritable museum of alchemical messages in this and other Notre Dame cathedrals.

The Grail as the Philosophers' Stone

When we consider Wolfram's poem, *Parzival,* where the Grail is described as a *stone,* we have no doubt he was talking of the *philosophers' stone.* This, together with other references to the stone being an emerald, the chivalric virtues shown by Firefiz (the result of a mix of cultures and faiths), the character of Trevrizent (Perceval's mentor and confessor, who was a hermit and not a priest), his insistence on the Grail story being of Oriental provenance, contained in a document found in Toledo, among other allusions, point to Wolfram being a Hermetic master within the stream of Rosicrucian thought. It was no coincidence that the wisdom of Hermes Trismegistus, in a collection of documents described as the *Corpus Hermeticum,* had reached Europe from Arabic sources during the period of the Crusades. It is therefore hypothesised that the true version of the story being of Islamic-Judaic origin and transmitted by the mysterious Kyot de Provence, was not to be taken literally, but as Wolfram's imaginative reconstruction of Hermetic truths.

The philosophers' stone of alchemy was the *prima materia* of creation, possessing superhuman or divine powers. It had the connotation of being precious or priceless because it was hard to find. The story that the Grail stone first appeared on the crown (or forehead) of Lucifer linked the Grail with similar jewels in eastern mysticism, like the emerald eye of Horus, the Schwarma of the Iranians, and the padma-mani of the Buddhists. These jewels were usually located at the mystic centre, often the forehead of the god, suggesting strongly the significance of this as a physical object standing for inner spiritual insight of the Third Eye. Identified mystically as the *pineal gland,* it is regarded as the bridge between the physical and material planes. This is the *stone* that facilitates mystical consciousness. In this stone, the spark of divinity could dispel the darkness of error and ignorance in mankind; for mankind, as a microcosm or the reflection of God, carries within itself the divine spark imprisoned in matter or its material body. Once its powers were understood and applied properly, the pineal gland could take mankind beyond the normally perceived limits of everyday reality. Mankind, in general, has lost the power to use the Third Eye, which makes the retrieval of the power, if sought after, much more difficult. Alchemically, this is the stone of wisdom, of the light, of understanding; it opens the "doors of perception." As such, the quest for the stone of wisdom should be seen as another quest for the Grail, it transforms people and confers unusual power. The Grail poets "initiated and revealed" by using the literary medium, the alchemist and the Rosicrucian used three other techniques: allegory of metals and their transmutation, the pictorial representation of the events happening in the alchemist's 'workshop', and finally, in written narrative, the replacement of the knightly quest by the mystic's quest.

Metaphors in Alchemy

Some examples, among many, will illustrate the points made above. The first example is the tract written by James Lacinus, A *Form and Method of Perfecting Base Metals* (c. 10 century) which, in a series of pictures, depicted the whole process of death and regeneration. A second example is to be found in the *Book of Lambspring,* the work of a 16th century alchemist. He takes up the Quest theme and shows the process of psychological transformation in several dramatic pictures, accompanied by short poems explaining each. As it would take too long to elaborate on the interpretation of these here, only a short summary of the message in Lacinus' work will be given. In the first picture, a Crowned King (the idealised or archetypal form, symbolising also the purity of Gold, the higher nature, or the perfected person) is surrounded by his son (Mercury) and five servants (the different impure metals, or people at various levels of consciousness). In subsequent pictures, we see the King, this divine being, enter into matter; it is a descent or degeneration. This is shown as the killing of the king by the son who is urged on by the servants, and the entry of both into a coffin. In alchemical terms it is an amalgam of gold and mercury being prepared, and the 'black' stage is reached. A grave is dug, meaning that the furnace is prepared to produce the heat required for effecting the chemical change required. The bodies are left to decay and putrefy in the casket. In the final picture, the Father is restored to life and the King's Son is made King through the regenerative process. The secret behind all this is that the right processes were carried out to activate the miraculous qualities of the *stone,* the transforming agent.

By analogy, we are witnessing in this *experiment,* the Grail King, the Ailing Grail King (the perfect one entering into matter), the inferior and unhappy condition of its people (the servants), Perceval as the Son (who in the Grail myth is related to the Ailing King), the suffering of the Grail King as he agonises with his unhealing wound (he waits for the amalgam of which Perceval is a part), the ordeals and spiritual turmoil experienced by Perceval as he seeks the Grail (the component of mercury that mixes with the degenerate gold in the otherworld of the grave), and his final attainment of Grail kingship in a happier Grail Kingdom (the King, son and servants wearing crowns). Psychologically speaking, if we regard the self as the Grail at the beginning of our quest to wholeness, both the myth and the alchemical allegory describe the condition of the human psyche as *impure* or unbalanced because of ego dominance in our lives. The self has to regain its royalty through the alchemical process or the quest through the adventure land of the unconscious.

The Mount of the Philosophers

The 16th century plate known as the *Mons Philosophorum,* with its captions and remarks, found in the collection of the *Secret Symbols of the Rosicrucians of the 16th and 17th Century* provides us with a third example (see Appendix 3). It is a single, complete picture of the alchemical and Grail quest. Its interpretation, attributed to Walter Stein and paraphrased by Ravenscroft, and interspersed with the writer's own additions, is summarised here (see page 139). The *Mount of the Philosophers* features a natural mountain landscape, complete with animal and human life, the sun, moon, and the results of human activity. The three persons at the bottom of the picture are three knights, Perceval, Gawain and Firefiz, in Wolfram's version of the Grail romance. They stand ready to make the initiatory journey to the highest level of consciousness. The naked man in the cave is Trevrizent, the wise hermit whom Perceval meets prior to his final visit to the Grail castle: he represents naked truth and the wise man archetype in its spiritual dimension. It is to be noted also that Trevrizent is Wolfram's construct of Thrice-Great Hermes (*Tre* = three, *zent* is equivalent to scientia = knowledge, science; three aspects of knowledge). The path winds its way to the top, the path to the Grail, the journey to the Alchemical Wedding. On this path the initiate or the Grail knight encounters various animals and significant events: they represent symbols of the trials and temptations experienced by the quester and the change processes occurring in his character. The fleeting thoughts of the seeker are represented by the hare; warmth and will power by the hen on a nest of eggs; pleasure and aversion of feeling, unleashed instincts, impulses and desires by the lion and the dragon; the entrapment of the soul or self is shown by the sun and moon in the dustbin; the alchemical changes that occur to the soul and spirit under the stress of fire is depicted by the cookhouse with the smoking chimney. This is close to the summit of the mountain, closer to the heavens, where the weight and bulk of the world of forms diminish, and the view panoptic. Having passed the test of fire, the initiate or knight is able to be less of a Fool, less dependent of social constraints to guide his conduct, and act more authentically. He is guided by intuition, can distinguish between the morally real and unreal, always acting with compassion, tolerance, and equanimity. He is now at the mountaintop, having earned his privilege of ascending Montsalvat, and being able to reach the top by acquiring self-knowledge through compassion. Above the mountaintop appear the symbols of the sun and moon, they have been delivered from their miserable state in the dustbin; they appear as such only at the appropriate level of consciousness of the quester. Now, in their orientation in the sky, they are the sign of the Grail, symbolized by the dove flying from the sun to the crescent moon, This recalls the dove in Wolfram's *Parzival*, which brought down the host on Good Friday to the Grail on earth, to renew the power of the Grail. The symbols of royalty at the peak indicate the arrival of the initiate before the Grail, the arrival at his or her inner centre, the *axis mundi*, where the whole universe is centred in mystical consciousness, where the self and the Greater Self are one.

Journey of Christian Rosenkreutz

Finally, we find alchemy reverting to the literary medium of the Grail romances. Two instances are worth recording. The first is the *Roman de la Rose*, written by Lorris and de Meung in the 14th century. This work can be interpreted, says Serge Hutin, "as an exaltation of the Mystical Great Work and the discovery of the philosophers' stone, by means of which the human soul attains after many ordeals, the perfect serenity of initiation ... The rose symbolises divine grace and the stone" (55). In the second instance, the knightly quest is replaced by an alchemical drama in prose, the main character being the alchemist himself. The work entitled *'The Alchemical Wedding of Christian Rosenkreutz'* opens with Christian in his study or laboratory, in a hut on a lonely hillside. It is a wild, stormy night, and he senses that he is in the presence of some great danger. He is suddenly visited by a huge angel, who manifests in an orb of blinding light. He is dumbfounded and fearful. This is his Grail visit, and he reacts as the Knights of the Round Table did on the first visit of the Grail in their midst. Then comes the act of love or grace, for in that moment of illumination he is given an invitation to attend a Royal Wedding, and the angel disappears. From that moment, having passed his first test as a result of diligent study and the practice of true alchemy, humbled by this experience and spurred on by hope, he commences his bewildering journey to the Nuptials (the final enlightenment) in which he is the unconscious participant. This allegorical journey, then, is the Rosicrucian and alchemical equivalent of the Grail Knight on the Grail Quest. It is full of symbolic meaning and rich imagery, and a masterful presentation of the initiatic tradition.

As a part of this tradition, modern Rosicrucians pursue a symbolic or knightly mystical quest. They work alone, work on themselves, self-analysing, seeking truth in the inner resources of their mind, responding to the urges of their hearts, as they seek to make the amalgam of their outer experience in the world and the wisdom of intuitive knowledge gained in reflection and in meditation. This is a patient and demanding process, yet exciting and full of adventure. As they gradually acquire the understanding that proceeds from self-initiation, they reach higher levels of consciousness. Then do they, without deliberate intent and unwittingly, become the object of observation by others, at that point when transformation has taken place. They attract such attention by simply being what they are, the refined golden metal, one who has drunk from the cup, those whose *stone* throws a blaze of light to illumine the path of those who follow.

Chapter 7

Symbols and Archetypes of the Grail Quest

The Perceval story has specific symbolic motifs or dominant themes which, in psychological terms, can teach us much. As is the case with most myths, we can use it as a means of understanding our individual nature and that of humanity as a species, since it encapsulates a considerable part of mankind's aspirations and experiences and throws lights on the mystery of life itself. Before proceeding with a psychological analysis, it might be helpful to summarise the story here.

Perceval the Welshman

Following her tragic experiences in a world of conflict, where she loses her kinsmen, Perceval's mother retreats to a forest home, taking the boy with her. There he is brought up in a natural environment, in isolation from society. As he grows into a youth, he becomes skilled in the use of the javelin, learns basic Christian values from his mother, shows a sensitivity to the contrast of necessity and beauty (the killing of a bird and the loss of the bird's singing), but his inexperience in the social world later gives him the character of a brash, innocent Fool.

One day he meets a few of Arthur's knights in the forest. He mistakes them for angels, as they wore shining armour, splendid regalia, and were bursting with power and masculinity. Having identified themselves, and following a short exchange of words, he suddenly gets the urge to become one of Arthur's knights. At home, he states his resolve to leave, despite his mother's protests. She dresses him in the poorest garb, in the hope that subsequent social ridicule would make him turn back. He then leaves her, and keeps riding on even when, on looking back, he sees her fall in a swoon. She actually dies heartbroken.

On the way he meets the "lady in the tent", forces his attentions upon her, robbing her of her ring, and further insults her before leaving. He does not know that all this would cause her to suffer from her husband, who misconstrues the whole incident. Later, Perceval reaches Arthur's court and gracelessly asks to be made a knight. Opportunity knocks! A Knight in Red Armour had just previously insulted the King, seized a golden cup from the table, spilt some wine on the Queen's dress, and was waiting defiantly outside for some reaction. Perceval immediately rushes out of the court to engage the knight, and brings him down ignominiously with his javelin. Then, donning the armour of the Red Knight over his lowly garb, he proceeds to act as a knight-errant.

He later meets Gournemanz, an experienced knight who teaches him courtly behaviour and the code of knightly combat, and shortly after he meets Blanchefleur, falls in love, and marries her. These events in his life, and his reflection on them, reduce his naïvete, increase his awareness of the feelings of others, and awaken in him a sense of responsibility. He decides to return home to comfort his mother, unaware of her death. But circumstances intervene. His destiny is being decided elsewhere — he is to be the Knight of the Grail, and it would appear that some unknown power is drawing him, unawares, towards the Grail Castle.

On his way back he comes to a river, where he meets a fisherman in a boat, who invites him to stay at his castle and directs him to find his way across upstream. When he crosses he finds himself in the "Otherworld" of the Grail. At the Grail Castle he is treated to a banquet provided by the Fisher King (the man in the boat), who has an enduring wound in the groin. He also witnesses a strange procession, in which a Grail Maiden carries a wondrous object called the Grail which dazzles everyone and also supplies everyone with the food they most desire. Accompanying the Grail Maiden is a youth carrying a lance that bled from its point, the drops of which fell onto his hand. Perceval was expected to ask a question such as "Whom does the Grail serve?" or "What ails thee, Uncle?", but does not. He does not know it at the time, but asking such a question would give him the power to heal the King's wound, restore fertility to his barren land and happiness to his people. He fails in this task because he misunderstood Gournemanz' instruction on when to ask questions; in other words he is not ready for the test.

The following morning, he finds himself alone in the castle, and on his departure the castle disappears altogether. The shock of the event on his feelings saddens him so much, that he loses his belief in God. He is doomed to wander about giving his horse free rein for another five years, before he meets a hermit who helps him understand himself better. The hermit initiates him into the nature of the Grail, and takes him to the Grail Castle. This is his final initiation before he is allowed entry into the Grail Castle. The same events are enacted in the castle as occurred in his first visit. This time he asks the question, the King is healed, and the Kingdom recovers. The old King dies shortly after, and Perceval becomes the Grail King.

Jung's Concepts of Human Nature

For the purpose of psychological analysis we need to briefly look at Carl Jung's concepts about the human personality. Jung used the term *psyche* to mean the total personality, which encompasses what is generally called the *mind.* He described the latter as being composed of two segments, according to its structure or behaviour at the conscious or unconscious levels. The unconscious is a storehouse of primitive instincts and impulses as well as of the collective experiences of humanity which have been repressed, forgotten or ignored by the conscious segment. Our behaviour reflects this split, when we admit that our acts are rational or irrational, yet we yearn to bring some rationality into our behaviour. The answer lies in our ability to release the unconscious experiences, which often are the source of unpredictable, inexplicable, or anti-social acts, from the unconscious to the conscious mind, and deal with them appropriately. The degree to which this is done determines the state of psychic or mental health of any individual. Failure to come to terms with the unconscious leaves the individual in a disordered state. It can be assumed then that all people remain at some point in the spectrum between disintegration and wholeness.

Some understanding of the dynamics of the unconscious is the first step towards "healing', or achieving integration. A major characteristic of the collective unconscious (the experiences that individuals carry with them as part of their heritage, as part of the human species) is its myth-making function. This function in earlier societies was their form of scientific thinking, which attempted to explain the facts of the world and its underlying order. In early societies the re-enactment of the myth, individually and collectively, provided the necessary therapeutic element to stabilise social life by giving individuals identity with their group and a meaningful place in their natural environment. In our day, the unconscious has undergone sufficient analysis, in an attempt to clarify certain mysteries of our nature, to enhance our understanding of what the ancients tried to do in other ways.

Jung tells us that primordial images, which humanity inherited from its ancestors, operating at the psychic level, make us react in certain ways to certain life situations. These behavioural patterns or predispositions to act in these ways he called archetypes. The objects of the archetypes (like images of snakes, the sea, the moon, trees, etc) were part of the language of the unconscious and revealed the nature of these archetypes. In the Grail myth, we find several of these images, e.g., sword, spear, stone, river, forest. The context in which they appeared or the way they were put together carried a message in symbolic form. These symbols in their positive and negative character reveal the nature of the archetypes at work. The aim of putting these together, if we are to be self-healers, is "to integrate the unconscious content into everyday experience, to drag the dark, irrational feelings and intuitions into the light of rational consciousness, and thereby extend the boundaries of the rational mind." (Chetwynd, xi). The most important archetypes, among many others, are the shadow, the animus/ anima, and the self. These, as well as others like the Wise Old Man, the King, and the Fool, appear in the Grail Myth.

Grail Myth as a Psychological Process

Myths, like that of the Grail, express the attempt of the psyche to balance and harmonise the energies of the two segments of the mind, the conscious and unconscious, and so sanitise the whole person. At the level of society, the achievement of psychic harmony in most of its members must reflect very positively on the state of society. In this chapter we shall pay more attention to the individual side; in the next we shall concentrate on the collective aspect.

Perceval's story starts in the forest in the mountains of Snowdonia, in Wales. The forest is the first image we meet, an important symbol. The forest nourishes and protects those who live within it. It rises out of the earth, flourishes on it, and its trees return eventually to the Earth Mother. New trees then continue the life of the forest. Perceval's mother chose it as the boy's home. Together, the mother and child is the symbol of mothering and nature at the human level. In the forest the child is close to the Earth Mother, and for a while is totally under her influence. The father's model of masculinity, the solar god, is masked by the canopy; that is, the influence of the conscious mind, is almost absent. So Perceval's horizons are limited in a somewhat lonely existence. The break from this had to come some time in his youth, and the trigger for this in the story was his encounter with five of Arthur's knights in his forest home. This could be described as Perceval's first Grail experience — the shining knights mistaken for angels — which sets his enthusiasm alight. This is an inner call, but being so young and solely under the control of the unmediated ego, his further encounters in the human world characterise him as the Fool, but an innocent one, not a clown.

There are few of us who are not like Perceval in our early years. We do not recognise our own foolishness and ignorance, and are often inconsiderate in our relationships. His Grail journey, of which he was not aware at this stage, must enable him to make two most important discoveries about his nature, discoveries made through his own effort. He has to find out the nature of his masculinity in the father-figures he meets, and he has to rediscover within himself the eternal feminine, the *anima,* described as the archetype of the soul.

Perceval's confrontation with the *Red Knight is* a confrontation with his own shadow, an archetype which represents the darker side of his nature, his raw undisciplined emotions. The violent repression of the shadow element in himself, was an over-reaction; it hindered the development of his conscious personality. We repress or disown the shadow because it interferes with our *persona* image. The inevitable consequence of this repression increases the potential for conflict in the psyche, as the shadow element attempts to recover from this repression. The fact that he puts on the armour of the Red Knight indicates that the shadow is still with him. The main outlet for reducing conflict, of reducing this energy innocuously, depends on the degree to which ego control is successful in managing it. Each decision has its consequences. Acting out (eg., killing because one hates) and projection (letting one's own acquisitive tendencies condition one's perception of society as corrupt), releases the energy, but does not solve the problem. Social reaction to these would introduce new problems for the psyche. On the other hand, sublimation (finding socially acceptable or tolerable means of "letting off steam", or cognitive restructuring of situations of stress) is a form of adjustment, of reconciling pressure from the shadow.

Healing Psychic Splits

There are other splits within the psyche which tend to keep us less than healthy. A most important imbalance is that of the unequal status accorded to the *anima* and *animus* archetypes. These are the masculine and feminine principles affecting the quality of human nature. In fact the Quest of the Grail is seen by some writers as essentially the attempt to heal this split between the masculine ego and feminine unconscious in the psyche.

Our next image in the Perceval story is that of the *persona* or mask. Here, the Red Knight's armour plays a second role to that of representing Perceval's shadow. For it is also symbolic of his new, adopted status. He puts on the armour over his lowly garments, which indicates that he is not yet a knight simply a role-player; for underneath, no real change has taken place. Most people wear a mask, it is their protection against the hardness of reality, as they see it. This is a necessary and temporary phase in people's growth as a social animal, namely the process of socialisation by experience or instruction. Wearing a mask gives a certain social identity and facilitates social interaction. One feels less of a fool and has some respectability. But the persona also has its negative side. Over-identification with it means that one can live superficially, cultivating a false ego, and deliberately stifling what is of value in the unconscious, in the inner self.

To a large extent, when Perceval visits Gournemanz' castle, his training to be a knight strengthens his persona without inflating it. His hitherto unbridled instincts are being tamed, as his mentor teaches him the social graces, the value of consideration of others, and the need to follow one's own intuitions with action. This initiatory sequence gives him a different perspective of his earlier behaviour at Arthur's court, his method of dealing with the Red Knight, the severe break with his mother and his rough treatment of the lady in the tent. He comes to realise that his manner of dealing with those situations is interfering with the direction he is taking in his life. In initiation ceremonies, initiates are always guided by a master or father figure who are examples or mentors who guide them through the various stages of the spiritual journey, or point the way to integration. They appear in many myths as the *Wise Old Man* archetype. In the Grail Myth, Gournemanz is the model for social graces and noble conduct, the Grail King presents a perfect masculine form, or the Wounded King an emasculated or degenerate role; and the hermit at the final stage in the quest gives this archetype a spiritual dimension. Generally, these figures symbolise the hidden meaning behind the apparent chaos of life, they represent the collective experiences of humanity facing repetitive situations that condition its development.

Grail Kingdom as the Unconscious

It is in his changed condition that he is able to find love, and marries Blanchefleur. This would be the moment of the sacred marriage, when his male/female components are in perfect harmony. Other events however seemed to be guiding his life. He has to leave his wife, to see his mother, but the return journey is interrupted as he comes upon a river, where he meets the strange Fisherman and is directed to the Grail Castle. The river is an important universal symbol. In this story it represents a frontier to be crossed into another territory, a mysterious world, the world which comes upon us unawares, the realms of dreams and visions, a magical world. Across the frontier lies the Kingdom of the Grail. But it is our world, the world of the unconscious. That is why it is so hard to find; now we see it, now we don't! When we do experience it, that is, when we can reach into the unconscious, it opens the way to the mysteries of our being. Anyone who enters the realm of the Grail, this otherworld, this invisible world, may experience joy or distress. But one can also return from it, somewhat changed.

Within the Grail castle, five symbols worked together to indicate the progress of Perceval's transformation. He is given a sword as a gift indicating a sign of growing discrimination in judgement and the strength to prevail over the dragons of the dark side of his nature. The spear dripping blood symbolises the wounds of the divided psyche, it breaks through resistance in the "old" personality. Upon his arrival at the banquet *the Queen covers him with her cloak*. This is a softening-up process, he recovers something he had known and lost in his childhood, a tempering of his masculine nature takes place. This is followed by the arrival of the Grail Maiden. Both these ladies represent the most positive aspect of the *anima,* the unconscious mediator of the true Self. The Maiden bears the Grail, which is spirit, which is to perform the miracle of transformation.

But that is not yet to be. He fails to ask the question, his understanding of life is still too limited. Even his social training holds him back, He was told not to ask too many questions in polite company, but he asks no question at all. His inner impulse to act genuinely on that occasion stumbles as he hesitates. The privilege of witnessing the Grail in the Grail Procession could be described mystically as a foretaste of enlightenment, or psychologically, as the self acquiring preeminence over other energies of the psyche. That nothing further happened and everything disappeared is a way of describing the abrupt return from the unconscious, without the process of psychic harmony being completed.

The Dark Night

Perceval has to meet the alchemical test of heat and 'blackness', or the mystical 'Dark Night of the Soul' in order to reach purification. He faces a period of disappointment, despair, and a loss of faith; and he is doomed to wander about the wilderness for another five years. Asking questions at moments of passage or turning points of our lives may be the secret to understanding the nature of the Grail. If we wish to seek our own Grail, that is, if we want to let our true self shine through, we must be prepared to ask questions like these: "Whom does the Grail serve?", "What's life all about?", "Where am I heading? . ... .. Am I ready to undertake the journey?", `What must I sacrifice, and am I ready to do it?", "What hindrances are keeping me from the Quest?" Questions like these mark the point of readiness for a particular initiation or that state of readiness of the psyche to adjust its dynamic. One of Perceval's later "adventures" illustrates the sort of change that occurs, drawing attention to the interplay of archetypes, in this case between the negative anima and the shadow. A woman asks Perceval to kill a Black Knight who lies in his tomb. Normally, it would have been an easy task to please the feminine anima and terminate the knight's life. But his past initiatory experiences had the effect of changing his response to these competing archetypes. The "wise old man" mediates, he takes on the feminine and wins: Perceval prefers to invite the Black Knight out and make friends with him. It is the Ego, now sufficiently discriminating and responsive to the archetypes, reflecting the qualities of the inner self. Perceval is moving closer to inner peace.

After years of wandering in the state of the 'dark night' or psychic chaos, Perceval meets the old hermit. Through him Perceval learns that striving is the way to find the Grail, but it would not be enough without the experiences resulting from his tenacity of purpose to bring changes to his nature. Not only has he to use discrimination in judgement (the sword), to thrust accurately (with the spear) to transfix ego dominance, and open to the power of love and compassion (the Grail Maiden), but he has to let go of the reins of his horse at times and let the animal (his intuitive nature) take him where it will. One has to yield to a power bigger than oneself, a power which some would say, is the Grail, or the Greater Self.

Chapter 8
Fisher King and Wasteland

We shall now examine the two symbols, the *Fisher King* and the *Wasteland.* Here two symbols go together, and form a myth within the Grail Myth, almost turning the purpose of the Quest from a search for a miraculous and sacred object to that of healing a king and restoring fertility to his lands. They give additional substance to the Grail Myth, however, making it a metaphor of the growth of the individual self, a description of the human condition in general, and how humanity relates to the environment

The Grail King in the legend holds his position by right of moral succession. He has to be the perfect man. But he has received a wound that never heals, which makes him also a Sick Grail King. He chooses to go fishing most of the time, and is therefore called the Fisher King. His land is barren, the waters have dried up, vegetation and animal life have disappeared, and his people are unhappy. The King can only be restored to health and the land to its former state of fertility by the visit of the Grail hero.

We may recall that the Guardian of the Grail, the Grail King, was sometimes represented in the Grail romances by two father figures, the Grail King ("the most beautiful person on earth"), and the Ailing King (the one with the incurable wound) brought into the banquet hall on a couch. Here the two persons represent a double aspect of the one person —what the King *should* have been, and what he was not at the moment of the hero's visit to the Grail castle. It is a similar situation to that described in the picture series of the Crowned King in the alchemical work of James Lacinus (mentioned in Chapter 6).

Meaning of Kingship

Let us deal with the meaning of the King symbol first. In the human consciousness, or if we use the terms of depth psychology, in the human psyche, *Kingship* is sought by the various archetypes. But it is the success of the archetype of the self in reaching this preeminent position in the psyche that enables the individual to reach a state of wholeness. The Ego, the centre or director of our conscious mind, inadequately or unworthily occupies the position of Kingship over the psyche, until the self, the force striving for unity of the whole psyche, attains royalty. When this happens, the psyche is then freed from disharmony, showing extreme health. The Ego, once strong but now weakened by psychic disharmony (the Sick King), is replaced by the Self (the Grail hero who becomes the new Grail King). Like the ideas found among the Rosicrucians and alchemists of the Renaissance period, the symbols of the Crowned King, the Sun and the metal Gold, are used in allegorical language to convey messages of the initiatory, mystical quest for fulfilment. In Alchemy, the search for the philosophers' stone was a search for the Grail. The real search behind the attempt to transmute physical metals into gold, was a quest for spiritual perfection. The King symbol was interchangeable with Gold, royalty among men and royalty among the metals. If the Grail King had become "impure" through some failure, the state was more concretely expressed in the impurity of Gold when mixed with baser metals. Both King and Gold had to submit to processes of alchemical change. The Grail King and Perceval must be seen as one person, illustrating the cyclic nature of the initiatory journey.

Symbols of Fish and Fisherman

Now, into this symbology of Sick King and Wasteland, another component is added — that of the *Fisher* King. The King takes on the character of a Fisherman, in which status Perceval meets him at the river. This interpolation seems to have entered the Grail Myth from a more general symbol in the human consciousness deriving from various sources. Vishnu's incarnation as a golden fish recalls his role as preserver and protector, like the Guardian of the Grail. Tibetan Buddhism sees the golden fish as being brought out of water from its experiences below the surface of the water into the light of liberation. The fish became a symbol of the early Christians, the sign representing Jesus as the saviour. Peter the Fisherman was the rock on which the future survival of Christ's teaching was assured, thus assuring the succession for the redemption of mankind, Jesus himself stated that he wanted his disciples to be "fishers of men." On the Celtic side, the Grail King Bran was associated with the sea and therefore, fishing. Finally, and even later than the period of the Grail poets, we find another example of alchemy, as depicted in one of the pictures in the *Book of Lambspring* of two fishes (soul and spirit) in the water (the body). There are some fishing vessels on the surface of the water. The thought of bringing the soul and spirit from their confinement in the world of experience suggests the liberating role of the Fisherman.

So the symbol became quite complex by the time the Grail Myth took shape, because of these contributing parts: the King, in his perfect or ailing condition; the role of fishing, in the sense of retrieving, saving or redeeming; and the watery depths of the unconscious, where the whole drama was to take place and where experience and wisdom were to be found. This background suggests more to the act of the Fisher King's fishing; other than that of being a mere pastime.

In the Perceval story, the Grail King is the father figure, whose responsibility it is to guide the kingdom of his whole being along the right spiritual path. He is "an ailing guide, however, who had long since lost his sense of direction and is now powerless to change the old order." In his wounded condition, he still has to hold together the whole kingdom (in a societal sense) and the health of his body (in an individual sense) under his care. He has done this well before, but now he is doing it badly. Life at the top (the head) is sick, therefore the rest (the body, land and its people), are out of harmony with it.

Myth of the Fall of Mankind

How the King and the Land got into this state is explained variously, either as the cyclic nature of events, or by simple accident such as wounding in battle, or the moral degeneracy of mankind (the Sick King as Fallen Man). Robert de Boron's Grail romance (c. 1200) indicates that the King is too old. If the kingdom suffered because he was unfit to perform as a competent ruler, then obviously a replacement was due. In some romances the "pure" Guardian of the Grail had done some wrong, either wilfully or thoughtlessly, earning himself an incurable wound in retribution. In the world of enchantment the wound would not heal, except under a specific condition. Seen from a mystical viewpoint, Ravenscroft explains the King's wound as symbolic of "perversion that has disrupted the blessed union of heart and brain (sic), and robbed him of all moral resolution." "Easy is the descent to Hell", the Roman poet Virgil wrote, but retracing one step is infinitely more difficult. Wolfram's Amfortas (the Grail King) had reached that low point; the bleeding lance used to cripple the King symbolised the terrible power of the unbridled instincts hindering the powers of the Grail.

The linkup between the King and the Wasteland is beautifully presented in the *Elucidation,* a continuation of Chrétien's story of Perceval. King Amangons, one of the successors of the Grail King lineage, once ruled a veritable paradise, called Logres. It was richly cultivated, prolific in bird and animal life, and provided all the necessities which made life pleasant for its people. The secret was that this paradise was kept watered by the Maidens of the Puis or Wells. Being the Kingdom of the Grail we could presume that the Wells themselves were sourced by the bountiful Grail, and the Maidens had a sacred task to keep the land fertile and also to refresh travellers throughout the land. Then one day King Amangons ravished one of the Maidens and stole her bowl. He set a bad example to his followers, who treated other Maidens in like manner. This was a violation of the sacredness of the land itself. It lost its fertility, animals became barren, trees became defoliated and bore no fruit and the land was eventually depopulated.

The metaphor is explained broadly in terms of mankind's general condition as the loss of natural grace. Wolfram's poem, *Parzival,* in taking up this theme, seems to be suggesting that mankind has split God from His Creation, by interfering with nature's laws and depriving it of its spirit. If this was mankind's mistake, then mankind had to correct it. The Grail King required the essential ingredient, for which he was fishing in the waters. It was there that he met Perceval and the recovery had begun. At first Perceval failed, he had only been driven by intuitions in various stages of the quest, but he needed to develop compassion. This happened on his second visit to the Grail castle when he asked the right question, "What ails thee, Uncle?" Perceval thus became the *"golden fish"* that saved the King and Land.

Our Woundedness

A comment by a Catholic writer on this aspect of the Perceval story is worth noting here. Referring to its message to the individual on the matter of personal growth and renewal, and a caution against the onset of anomie, he notes: "The Fisher King is what everyone moves into: death and emptiness and woundedness by the time we're fifty, if we have not walked Perceval's journey. He is a warning sign, a wake-up call, to people who are still young enough to change"

(Rohr, p.153). The Fisher King's problem is our problem, if we recognise the contradictions in our own nature and fail to transcend them. But the myth tells us that we also have the power to achieve this spiritual goal, with a little bit of help from the spirit of the Grail, once we start the journey.

We may perceive the Wounded King concept as a psychological lesson of growth, development, and fulfilment, with the Wound (psychic disharmony) acting as a running sore and also as a catalyst assisting growth towards healthy masculinity. The Wounded Fisher King symbolises the wound, says Robert Johnson, of every man in Western civilisation. It applies to the masculine element in women as well. Its expressions are to be seen in the persistent feelings of loneliness, anxiety, alienation, and inferiority, felt throughout life. The Wound was felt in the time of the Grail romances and it is felt even more so today. The seeds of this problem in the modem Western world were laid at the beginning of the second millennium, the transition period being the late Middle Ages, when the beginnings of modern science and the technology developing from it ushered in a world of material prosperity where materialism has become an idol. The wound occurred when the fetish of rationalism, of cool, clear, thinking, though a virtue in itself, suppressed the feeling function in man; the feeling function which had the capacity to better determine value, to develop a warmer relationship with nature and human nature, and to contribute to human happiness.

The answer to the problem or the healing of the wound, as suggested by the Myth, is to be found "in the most unexpected place, in the blunderings of an innocent fool ... inventive, capricious, youthful ... (but) ... who has it in his power to release the agony of the Fisher King" (R. Johnson, passim.). We are offered a vision of the meaning of life in our youth, but we fail to make it conscious and assess it properly. This was the reason for Perceval's failure to ask the Question at the Grail banquet. As he did, we too spend most of our lives in despair trying to find the Grail Castle again. Yet this is a necessary part of the psychological process — "the wounded part of ourselves can be left behind when it has served its function in the development of the mature man" (R. Johnson, p. 49).

Jean Bolen has the interpretation of this King/Land composite symbol as a prescription for healing the wounded or disturbed psyche in each one of us as a member of the species. She asserts that we are all wounded by being part of "a competitive materialistic society where cynicism towards spiritual values exist ... and the ego is cut off from experiencing the self' (p. 42). Our mistake, causing and maintaining the unhealing wound, is that of using scientific thinking as a rational principle and of cutting ourselves from the Grail, from spirituality, form intuitive feeling, The innocent young Fool of the legend is perhaps "the young, naive, innocent element within the psyche", only deemed foolish by the rational element, that can restore the connection between the ego and the Self. Bolen concludes: "The internal landscape, which has been a wasteland or dry desert may bloom or be green again, as emotional and spiritual feeling, the irrational elements in touch with the symbolic layer of the unconscious, are brought into the personality' (p. 43).

King and Wasteland Nexus

In vegetation or agricultural myths (and the symbols of the King and Wasteland in nexus makes the Grail story one of these), the King's health corresponds exactly with the quality of life in his domain. If we use the symbol to throw light on our understanding of human nature, we can see that two principles must work in harmony here: the King being the masculine principle, and the Land, with whom the Earth Goddess is associated, being the feminine principle. The dominant male principle, the King, was ailing, the land became a desert in sympathetic response, and the two principles were in disharmony. At an individual level, somewhere and at some time, the self had failed to respond to the intuitive call of the Greater Self, the call of the Grail. There, in the unknown background, the Grail was keeping the King alive, when he was losing hope, and it did not make him better. Yet it could not abandon him. It was waiting until he reflected, not on his degenerate condition, but on the virtues of the Grail, on the spirit of divinity within him. That part of him that finally awoke appeared in the form of the fully-matured Perceval.

The image of the *Wasteland* appears in myth to illustrate periods in history when kingdoms or civilisations suffered a decline or fall, or a sudden collapse. In the mythical explanation, since the mythic symbol connects the land and rulers causally, the ruler bears the guilt. The myth consequently promoted the idea of revival through renewal. A new king with a new zeal, morally unblemished, one in perfect control and driven by a new will, would therefore restore the kingdom to its former greatness and prosperity. We see this also in literature as the romantic yearning for the lost Golden Age.

But the King/Wasteland nexus may not be just myth, it may be part of human memory. For instance, we have the story of King Cadwallader of the Britons in the 7th century, who ruled peacefully from his accession, and then after twelve years, became ill. Being unable to function as an effective ruler, dissension broke out among the Britons, and the ensuing civil strife turned the kingdom into a wasteland. Again, the pattern is represented in Arthur's reign as a real historical event, without the additional gloss of legend. The cycle commenced with war and disorder in the land, moved into a quarter century of peace and justice in a united realm, to the final collapse of Arthur's rule and the return to barbarism.

On the other hand, the Wasteland is depicted as a social and natural phenomenon spread over a few centuries rather than a condition of the land before or after the appearance of a specific historical royal figure. In this case, the Wounded Fisher King and the Wasteland images become an allegorical representation of the religious and political tensions prevailing in Britain of the Dark Ages, beginning at the time of the last Roman legion (AD 410) to the period of the Grail romances (12th - 13th centuries). The religious conflict was between Celtic and Roman Christianity, the former seeking to resist doctrinal domination by the latter. The contest began about the time of the Pelagian heresy (AD 416) described as challenges to the authority of the Church of Rome on the questions of free will and original sin, and the nature of the apostolic succession, which had to be settled. The concept of the Wounded Fisher King in legend stood for the weakening, and later incurably wounded, Celtic Church, when its long-standing resistance to Rome was finally settled at the Synod of Whitby (AD 664).

The Wasteland in this context was occasioned by three factors: the Celto-Roman religious conflict, the threat of civil disorder caused by Saxon incursions into British territories, and natural events like the bubonic plague which swept Europe in the mid 6th century. At the time, the Kentish (Saxon) kings were trying to establish Augustinian dominance over the faith of the English, there was considerable confusion and anxiety among the English at the rumour that the

Grail was the "true body of Christ." `Was the Grail something Celtic or Roman?" was the hidden question behind Perceval's question at the Grail Castle "Whom does the Grail serve?". We must assume that the Grail romances were not only a key to the existence of a mystery tradition but also, or alternatively, an indirect political statement of a subversive content raising the question of one set of religious teachings against another. Did the Grail serve a Celtic Fisher King who represented Celtic Christianity (wounded in the religious conflict) or else an authority external to Britain and centralised at Rome? Mike Ashley, who argues along these lines concludes: "there was considerable illness in the land and the Fisher King was ailing. No wonder there was yearning from the Celtic Church to restore the King and help the land" (Ashley, Introduction p. 8).

The Grail story reflected the dilemma of the few centuries preceding its emergence in the 12th century. Among its various themes, one that was stressed was the question: "Was the Church of Rome the real harbour of the Church of Christ, or did it rest firmly with the British?" (Ashley, Ibid). The hero, Perceval, and the healing of the Fisher King was therefore pointing to the resolution of the problem. In fact it did not. It only left the problem for posterity. Rome asserted itself again, though not in an official capacity, but through the work of the Cistercian clerics who produced the Vulgate cycle of the Grail romances. In this, the linkage of the Grail with the blood and body of Christ, the creation of a new Grail hero, Galahad, and the idea of the Grail being removed from the eyes of people forever, neutralised the effectiveness of this Celtic strand. The nature of this tension has come down to us in the 21st century in the form of the pagan Goddess vs. a Christian patriarchy as polarised modes of thought expressing western spirituality.

On a broader canvas, Godwin argues very cogently that the Golden Age which literature extols (an Age in which there was no Wasteland, nor unhappy people, and their rulers were not tyrants), may have been a historical reality in periods long before the Christian era. This paradise is not what most of us are led to believe, namely that this beatific state exists only as a utopia created in people's minds by the despair at the human condition and the hope for what ought be if only people were different.

Archaeological evidence points to the existence of Neolithic agricultural paradises existing in Turkey, the Balkans, and Southern Russia, where societies lived side by side, and violence seemed to be unknown (the absence of weapons of war), although skilful domestic objects and tools, small altars and sacral vessels were found in various sites. He suggests a preeminence of an Earth Goddess in their beliefs, from the figurines and other artefacts discovered, a life-giving spirit that permeated community life which supported values of equality and cooperation, and that this agricultural phase most probably was the result of the way history developed among many of the later *civilised* societies. Perhaps, these societies were overcome by hunter tribes, and the people affected by this shock despairingly dreamed of their former state of joy and peace, which became the substance of legend. He concludes that the Grail myths echo a catastrophe like this, recalling the event in the collective unconscious. We may see this in the Celtic and Christian myths, where paradise was to be regained by a Grail hero or Christ figure (Godwin, p.24).

A Myth for Modern Humanity

Regardless of the sources, the finding of which has been an exciting experience, the myth has become part of our unconscious, surfacing spontaneously from time to time into consciousness when natural and historical circumstances in the world of history set off a trigger. We can still see some truth revealed in the myth of the Ailing King and the Wasteland, when applied to our own situation in this day and age. We often ask, as we contemplate our survival as a species, if our own catastrophe is already here or almost upon us, which provokes lively debate on value systems on human purpose and destiny, as one interprets warnings on the state of the planet.

We, as the human species, may be that Sick King, and the Wasteland our home. We have made it that way! Whether we are a small group, an organisation, a country, or the human race, we could be reliving the symbol. Some would say that events are predetermined anyway, we are experiencing some great cycle of events, there is very little we can do about it. Others counter with the assertion that we have free will, we can make choices, and we can turn the tide. Is it possible that the time has come when no choices but one course remains? And it certainly will not be that which absolves us individually from any responsibility. If our neglect, wastefulness, and destructive thoughts, have presented us with the problem of extinction in an overburdened world, then the process must be reversed somehow. And so, as hopeful people we can turn to the Grail for its *miraculous power*. We are told, in this Sick King/Wasteland theme of the Grail myth, that the Grail sustains life in the expectation of the arrival of the Grail hero, that is, in the expectation of change in the human spirit. Change this, and you bring back the spirit to the land. The voice of the Grail spreads the message of love for the Earth and its creatures. If this message is translated into action, the health of the Earth will be restored.

Perceval's quest for the Grail, seen in this context, represents the role of mankind and its leaders, guided by new sets of ideals, revivified by the experiences of the past. As a species, we are a wounded people. We have to do our fishing and go on fishing and nurse our wounds rather than grieve for them. Then one day, answering the intuitive call of the Grail the Fool/Hero will appear at the bank of the river, and later, before it is too late, heal our wound and restore the land.

The Pelican was an alchemical symbol of re-vivification, sometimes seen as regurgitating its food to feed its young, and sometimes as the scaling of its breast to provide, sacrificially, the food (blood) of life. The symbol is appropriate to describe the Grail as Goddess through whom and by whom the hero achieves his quest.

Chapter 9

The Goddess and the Grail

There are a few modern writers who link the Grail Quest with the Quest for the Goddess, in its aspect as an archetype at work in the human psyche or as a numinous power at work in the cosmos necessitating human response. Although coinciding with the feminist movement, the writers are not all women. This trend seems to reflect a greater awareness of the feminine principle at work in human affairs.

As we examine this feminine principle as a theme in the Grail Myth, it would be prudent to indicate at this point that in this article masculine- feminine contrarieties or complementarities refer to metaphorical meaning applicable to psychic energies in man or woman, and not to gender specificity in biological or social roles. That the psychological state of disharmony has been reflected in, or projected into, gender-specific external and attitudinal positions in our society is an unfortunate legacy of the past. One of the great challenges that faces us today is to work at attitudinal change in the social environment (i.e., role modification and amelioration), and to achieve a balance of animus and anima energies.

Suppression of the Feminine

For hundreds of years, most societies have lived within the dominion of a male God and a dominant patriarchal organisation. Those societies that have made women inferior to men could not elevate the female principle — of the male/female polarities in nature — to an equal, balanced or complementary state with the male principle. The Goddess in mythology or religion performed a subservient role to a Supreme God in another transcendent or coexisting world of reality. And so, social life in these societies was ordered around this belief, with the male having a dominant role. It would be a truism to say that the major religions of the world, in some authoritative statements and in their practices, reflect this thinking. In Christian Europe of the later Medieval period, when a large number of Grail romances made their appearance, statements were made unequivocally that woman was the temptress, principally a child-bearer, inadequate to attain enlightenment, "impure" on occasions, or of infirm or imperfect character. Godwin explains that the thirst for the essentially female within myth — and he was specifically commenting on the Grail Myth — became more exaggerated and urgent, the more the church with its popular male hang-up about potent women, tried to repress her, as in the earlier attempts to repress the cult of the Virgin Mary.

Grail Mysticism Reflects Women's Empowerment

Attitudes are changing much faster in some societies and in some denominations of the religions of those societies. In other places reaction is hardening towards any change in women's status. It is not the purpose of this article to debate on the rights or wrongs of the values expressed and attitudes taken. In Medieval times, however, women were having a pretty rough time, ranging from status inferiority to burning for witchcraft. For a brief time, the light of the Grail spread by the troubadours and their female sponsors, like Eleanor of Aquitaine, Marie de Champagne, Marie de France, and Esclarmonde de Foix, shone brightly in the reconstructed legends of Arthur and his Round Table Knights. If the legends in any way represented a small change in the consciousness of man, it was significant. Here was an attempt to regain something that was once the dignity accorded to women in Megalithic and Celtic Europe. In those societies the Earth Goddess and the Solar Deity were seen as equal divine participants in the processes of creation and destruction. Celtic crosses, seen in the British Isles and Ireland in stone carvings and artifacts, or in Megalithic sites like the Callanish stones, represent symbolically a harmonious fusion of Christian and "pagan" symbols. The symbols show the ring of the Goddess encircling the heart of the Cross. It would appear as if a solar god and an earth goddess enjoyed a harmony in creation. In the Celtic crosses, sometimes the circles at the meeting of the arms are doubled or tripled, suggesting a vibrant emanation from the heart of the cross, like waves radiating outwards from the effect of a stone thrown into a still pool. This symbol itself preceded Christianity. The Avebury stones in Wiltshire, that huge engineering feat of the Megalithic builders, displays massive stones representing the male and female principles of creation. The long avenues are laid out in male and female pairs, equally matched; their shapes make it obvious.

Women's Status in Ancient Times

Homage to the female principle also surfaced about the time of Christ in the eastern Mediterranean, We note how the Gnostics placed great emphasis on the feminine wisdom of *sophia*, a sort of Grail Maiden. In their mystery ritual at *Eleusis* a ritual bowl was used. The pictorial art work on the bowl discovered there shows what appears to be the form of a Grail Maiden holding a bowl or *krater*. Here, it is a woman not a male figure, playing some important part in the Eleusinian rite. The esoteric explanation for feminine wisdom, the wisdom of sophia, was not that wisdom obtained by sensory observation and intellection, but by intuition in understanding oneself, and hence knowing about human nature and human destiny — a knowledge that comes from the heart (Bolen, pp. 254~5).

Archaeology has turned up evidence in prehistoric Europe and Western Asia of societies where long periods of peace were experienced. The "welding force which brought these peoples closer together ... was the Goddess ... Her name turns up in every aspect of daily life" in these early communities ... "The world was seen as female, and female was seen as the world ... But while the protective, procreating, and caring view of the world must have been dominant, the male, far from being inferior, must have been regarded as potentially essential to the health of the whole community" (Godwin p. 220). There was equality and shared responsibility, trust and mutual caring.

Woman's Role in the Grail Myth

Now the Grail myth can be seen as an attempt to recover this state of male-female balance. As a category of myth it seems to stand between the view that it is "one of the last great myths of masculine development", and that which makes it a story about the women of the land, the ancient goddess exerting power over men and events through characters and themes. In the Grail castle, the Grail Maiden, not a priest, was prominent in the Grail Procession. Even in the later Christian versions. the Grail Bearer was a female, one who was the "purest'.

Perceval breaks from his mother's influence, but not long after he wishes to return to her. The Hideous Creature (a female) chastises him to the point of making him abjectly guilty. Blanchefleur presents a model of resonance between his projected love object and the real thing, a marriage of true love that was meant to last. Lastly, the forest is the place of his upbringing and adventure, it is considered to be the unconscious when interpreting the symbols of myth, and psychologically the feminine is equated at times with the unconscious.

Accounts of the Grail Procession usually link the Grail with the *bleeding lance.* Following the lead of Jessie Weston, some writers often point to the vessel and the lance as sexual symbols. The pagan imagery of the lance being dipped first into a magic cauldron, was later replaced by a chalice and spear that pierced Christ's side. Being carried before the Grail, dripping blood from its point, showed that there was some symbolic or ritual value present. It is to be taken further, however, than an interpretation of the act of suffering and sacrifice of the Saviour. The Grail was the symbol of the womb of the Goddess, and its contents were the blood of life. The lance was the masculine element. When dipped into the contents, the lance carried the healing component. Mary thus becomes more than a heartbroken mother at the crucifixtion, giving more depth to the Christian mystery; The two objects, Lance and Grail, were both necessary in the healing process, the two basic elements (masculine and feminine) "uniting to restore the waste and infertile land of the Grail to its ancient richness and fertility" (Markale p.174). Grail Christianity and orthodox Christian doctrine would seem to reach a close consanguinity here (no pun was intended!).

One has also argued that the Quest itself is an expedition into the otherworld, a return to the womb "to recreate a state of paradise that preceded birth" (Ibid. p.174). The role of the Virgin Mary may be seen as a development of this idea. The Quest could be a return to God from the initial separation from It, and the adulation of Mary may be justified on the ground that she is a temple and vessel for the Divine, and as "one who mirrors the greatness of God".

Male or Female Quest?

These observations seem to favour the view that the "Grail is a female symbol, and that the Quest that the knight undertakes is a search for femininity" (Ibid). Which may tempt us, since the matter of gender roles today has a highly charged emotional component, to ask the question:—Why not a female knight on the quest?" The answer is to be found in some of the opinions expressed in the preceding paragraphs. It is said that men need the Quest, women do not. That is why they appear as Grail Maidens, Grail Messengers, as characters involved in various knightly encounters, who present difficult tasks for knights to perform, who counsel and admonish the hero, and so on. They act as initiatory guides to men, pointing the start of the journey, lighting the way, and facilitating the hero's successful completion of the Quest.

And they talk to us also, reminding us of the broader theme of man and his error. The *Lady in the Tent* episode in Perceval's first adventure shows insensitivity to the rights of others, his act of robbery (the ring), the extortion of kisses, and later insult suffered by the Lady. This points metaphorically to the desecration of the Temple of Jerusalem (the tent being the house of God sheltering the innocent), and also to the sin of Adam. The rest of the story is Perceval's (or man's) final success in rebuilding the Temple and restoring man's primordial state. Man's error is described, but a woman is the victim. Perceval has to evaluate the incident and all his later conduct against his experience of love for Blanchefleur, the chastisement of the Repulsive Creature, his gracious treatment by the Grail Queen, and his first initiation by the Grail Maiden into the secrets of the Grail.

This *initiating* role of women is to be seen in other Arthurian tales, the leading figures being Guinevere, Vivian and Morgan. They confer sovereignty on the male characters, tease or enchant them, sometimes making excessive demands on their good will, and caring for their wounds. They show the positive and negative aspects of the *anima* within the psyche of the heroes. If the Grail Quest is a story of separation from and return to our true nature, it is argued that women may not find it necessary or convenient to make this separation "because their wombs and bodies have closer ties with the natural cycles of life than men's". Against that, it is also argued that women do experience a necessary separation, in the processes of birth, life, death and resurrection as they "strive for fulfilment and completion on interior levels ... But for men, separation and isolation is simply the hero's natural state ... Men strive not for interior completion but for outer perfection." The outward hero's journey is not for woman as she has already integrated matter with the spirit, and she knows it. As Helen Luke puts it: She "has integrated the life of the spirit with the instinctive life of the flesh through living in the world at all levels of the love which is the way of conscious return to the unity of all opposites" (Matthews, p. 94).

As we focus on the positive and cosmic aspects of femininity, and we come to believe that the Goddess-Grail concept provides us with the most comforting explanation of the mystery, it still remains a mystery. We must not forget that, universally, myths have also presented images of women as the Terrible Mother or the Devouring Female, who eats up all children except her own. This is the negative, dark side of femininity which today sees the women's advocate stridently repeating that "there is only one truth, one way of feeling, one way of understanding", the woman's way, and that "all men are rotten, and domineering and militaristic, and all women are earth-mothers, and naturally creation-centred". (Rohr, p.68). This also includes possessive wives and extremely assertive women who have lost the caring, guiding civilising role in human relationships.

In their thrust directed at an enduring patriarchy, they paradoxically take on an over-charge of masculinity. The *animus,* or spirit element in dominance, has caused a diminution or displacement of the *anima* or soul element. In this case it would seem that the outward journey of the hero becomes, likewise, the hero's quest in woman. In our own time, this quest has started for some women who have become alienated from the "spiritually, psychologically, and nourishing Grail function of their womanhood ... they have lost their own Grail, and have to go in search of it just as men do, to find spiritual harmony" (Hansend, in Introduction to Evola, ix).

As far as the male is concerned, even as he goes after divine femininity, as he should, he has to live out his own role in the creative process. He must separate, thrust forward, learn the wisdom of trial and error "out there", seek to heal his father's wound (that is, his own wounded masculinity), and reach the Grail. For a man, healthy masculinity, not unmediated "machismo", should be the goal. He should discover experientially the feminine side of his being.

Some would say that the integration of the feminine is the most important process in the psyche which helps to form a bridge between ego and the self. This does not mean that men have to be regarded "merely as consorts to an all - powerful Goddess ... (but as) ... Warriors and Hunters by nature ... (who need) ... to do something that benefits the Earth Mother" (Kenneth Johnson, p.18).

The Goddess Keridwen

Chapter 10

The Dark Side of the Myth

We made reference earlier to Otto Rahn and his attempts to find the secrets of the Grail in southern France in the early thirties. This was the time when Hitler and his National Socialist Party were tightening their grip on the political apparatus in Germany, subsequently leading to the Second World War and the collapse of the Third Reich in 1945. Since the end of that low phase in human history, there have been reports collected from contemporaries of Hitler which reveal his interest and those of his cadre of SS officers in the subject of the Grail and the Round Table legends. They show, apart from Hitler's interest in the occult, how Nazi behaviour was conditioned to a certain extent, by the perverted perceptions of this ruling group, of the Grail, the spear that dripped blood, and the notions of the Grail guardianship.

The Spear of Destiny

What has come to be called the *Spear of Destiny* figured as a powerful symbol in Hitler's own philosophy, actually materialised in the form of a relic kept in the Hapsburg Museum. On the legendary side, it is known as the spear of Longinus, the compassionate Roman centurion who thrust his spear into the side of Christ between the fourth and fifth ribs, in order to end his misery. This act resulted in his being cured of his partial blindness, and established the magical (curative) properties of the lance. Before this Christianisation, the lance that appeared in the Procession at the Grail Castle, had magical associations derived from the Celtic background. It was of divine origin, never failing to miss its mark in conflict, sometimes having to be dipped in a magic fluid to maintain its poisonous or healing nature. It is represented also as a phallic symbol when associated with creativity, and again as symbolising intuitive judgement or the application of divine will. In the banquet hall of the Grail Castle, it was borne by a youth walking next to the Maiden who carried the Grail. In one version of the Grail myth, the hero, Galahad, heals the Fisher King's wound by applying the tip of the lance to it.

Mike Ashley assigns the spear to a different historical and symbolic context.

If it was the spear that caused the wound in the Perceval story, then it symbolically was the instrument of Roman Christianity wounding Celtic Christianity in Britain in the Dark Ages. The wounding of the Fisher King, representing Celtic Christianity, by the Roman Church, was a metaphor of the Celto-Roman conflict and its unsatisfactory resolution. Perceval's question, "Whom does the Grail serve?", says Ashley, had to relate to identifying the nature of that division. In this case, the spear no longer had the character of a merciful and healing instrument, so empowered by its contact with the heart of Christ, but one which was cruelly punitive and which was revisited in the tale of the Wounded King. Celtic Christianity had received the incurable wound, which had to be avenged (the Welsh Peredur story bore connotations of a vengeance theme). Presumably, the vengeance exacted would justly compensate for and so *heal* the wound, that is, restore the primacy of the Celtic Church. Ashley concludes: "The Quest for the Holy Grail became a quest to rescue the Celtic Church and to prove its preeminence over the Roman Church ... By their quest for perfection and ultimate redemption, the knights of King Arthur would establish the primacy of the Celtic Church ... (whose) ... quest very rapidly became the quest for each individual to search in his heart for an understanding of the true religion and to follow that course" (Ashley, Introduction.)

The spear used in this context then, has the attribute of vengeance, of finding compensation for the wound inflicted. Its use in this manner would restore the Grail to its rightful keeper. His wound would heal, the land would recover and its people be redeemed. So long as the spear worked for the Grail, it determined the destiny of those who wielded it. It gave power, it served God. Separate the Spear from the Grail, it would serve diabolical purposes and in the wrong hands, end in catastrophe.

The conjunction of the Grail as the chalice of the Last Supper and the container of Christ's blood, with the lance that was dipped in that same blood in the heart or container, was a powerful symbolic combination. Both objects were being related to the divine redeeming substance, forming the essence of life and the creative process. The sacredness and the punitive power of the lance is one of the high themes of Wagner's operatic presentation of *Parsifal* in which the divine will of God is demonstrated by the way the lance is used; it is finally used in conjunction with the chalice for healing the Fisher King. The condition of

Author's map showing the reported locations and movements of the Grail

The Ruins of Glastonbury Cathedral (*Author's Photo*)
Below left; Joseph of Arimathea.

The Taunton Cup. A replica of the Glastonbury Grail, bronze. It has a closer affiniy to the Celtic Cauldron than the Christian Chalice (*Author's Photo*)

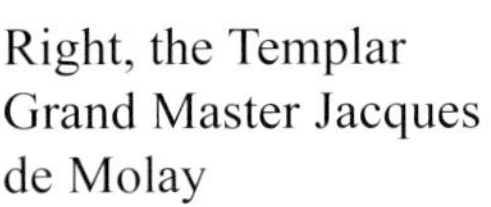

Right, the Templar Grand Master Jacques de Molay

Left, Two knights before a Grail Maiden

Grail procession and Fisher King

Left; The Templar Church, London.

Below; Templar Tombs at the Templar Church. *(Author's photos)*

Cathar monument at the base of Montségur (*photo courtesy Bob Kogel*)

The Grail Castle (*artist unknown*)

Setting out on the Quest for the Holy Grail

Neuschwanstein (1869-1886) Grail Castle built by Ludwig II of Bavaria (*Author's photo*)

The ruined castle of Montségur (*photo courtesy Bob Kogel*)

Castell Dinas Bran. A mountain with ruins of a medieval castle, near Llangollen. Welsh legend regards it as the Grail Castle. Dinas Bran is a few kilometres from the Snowdon Range where Perceval (Peredur) was raised. (*Author's photo*)

The Chalice Well at Glastonbury (*Author's Photo*)

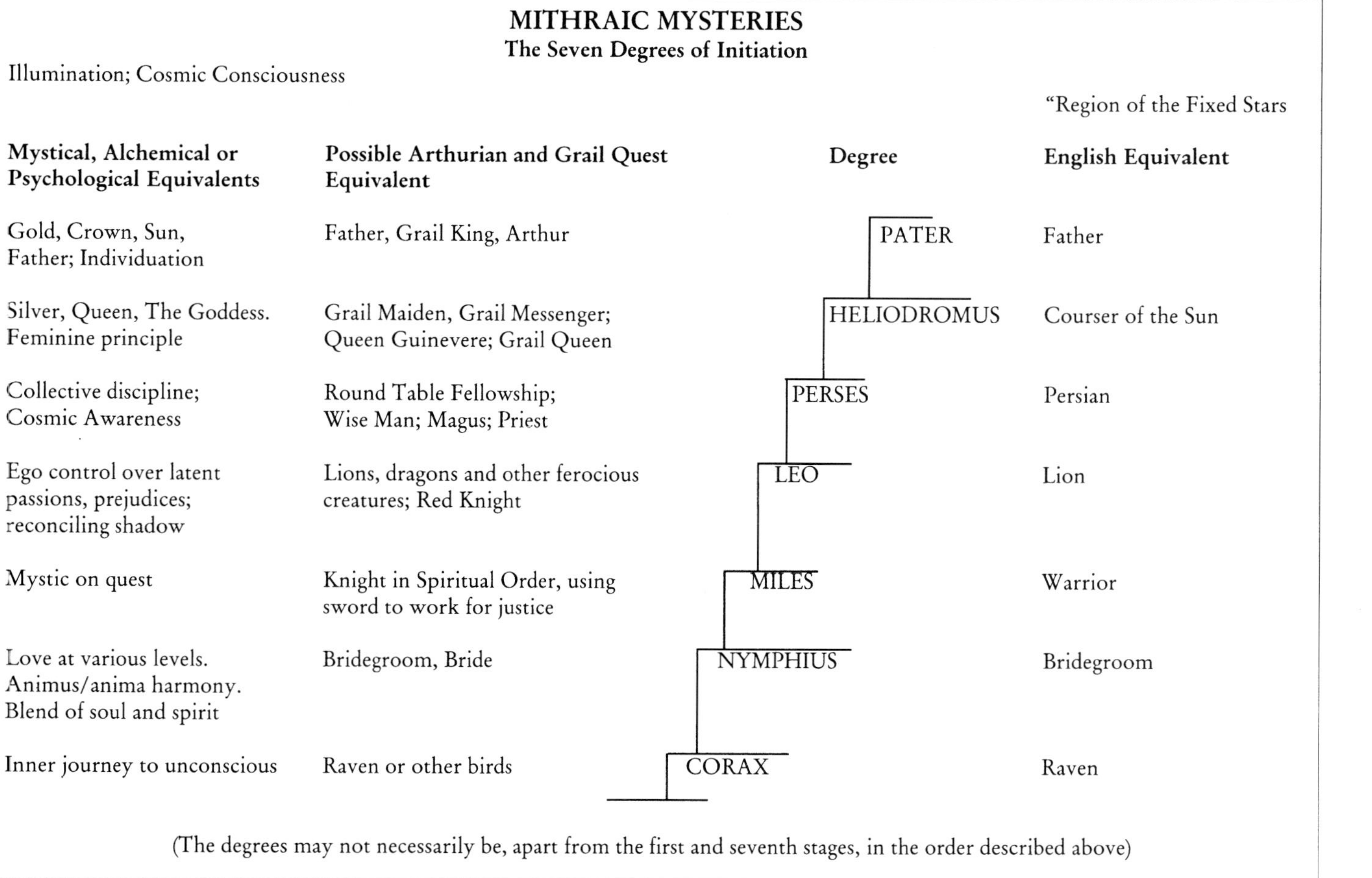

MITHRAIC MYSTERIES

The Seven Degrees of Initiation

Illumination; Cosmic Consciousness

“Region of the Fixed Stars

Mystical, Alchemical or Psychological Equivalents	Possible Arthurian and Grail Quest Equivalent	Degree	English Equivalent
Gold, Crown, Sun, Father; Individuation	Father, Grail King, Arthur	PATER	Father
Silver, Queen, The Goddess. Feminine principle	Grail Maiden, Grail Messenger; Queen Guinevere; Grail Queen	HELIODROMUS	Courser of the Sun
Collective discipline; Cosmic Awareness	Round Table Fellowship; Wise Man; Magus; Priest	PERSES	Persian
Ego control over latent passions, prejudices; reconciling shadow	Lions, dragons and other ferocious creatures; Red Knight	LEO	Lion
Mystic on quest	Knight in Spiritual Order, using sword to work for justice	MILES	Warrior
Love at various levels. Animus/anima harmony. Blend of soul and spirit	Bridegroom, Bride	NYMPHIUS	Bridegroom
Inner journey to unconscious	Raven or other birds	CORAX	Raven

(The degrees may not necessarily be, apart from the first and seventh stages, in the order described above)

Comper Lake in the forest of Brocéliande, where, according to local folklore, Lancelot was raised by Viviane the fairy goddess below its calm waters in the Celtic Otherworld
(*Author's photo*)

Chartes Cathedral. The Southern Portal
(*Author's photo*)

Newgrange, County Meath. Photo reproduced by kind permission
National Monuments and Historic Properties Service, Ireland

Inside Newgrange. Photo reproduced by kind permission
National Monuments and Historic Properties Service, Ireland

The Proto-Grail in the heart of the Newgrange monument. Photo reproduced by kind permission National Monuments and Historic Properties Service, Ireland.

Silbury Hill
A massive man made mound built by Neolithic people in celebration of the Goddess. An aerial view reveals the shape of a squatting (pregnant) Goddess in the central mound and surrounding marsh. (*Author's photo*)

The Wewelsburg Castle
Photo reproduced by kind permission of
Kreis Paderborm

Right, The Spear of Destiny, picture reproduced from Trevor Ravenscroft's *The Spear of Destiny*, Samual Weiser, 1982. Permission to reproduce granted by Samual Weiser inc.

Stonehenge, view from the west showing the altar stone. (Author's photo)

The Knights of the Round Table experience the Grail Vision. *Manuscript Illustration c 1470*

Amfortas as the Ailing Grail King and the unhappiness of the Grail Kingdom, as revealed in the music-drama, is caused by the King's moral lapse, leading to the loss of the spear to Klingsor, the magician. It was used improperly, and was eventually captured by the "Fool", Parsifal, who brought it back to the Grail castle and used it along with the contents of the Grail, to heal the King. A mystical explanation of this interprets cup and spear as the union of understanding (the cup), and the will or wisdom (the spear), which alone is capable of enlightening it (the cup) perfectly. At one moment in the drama, Parsifal thrusts the sacred spear into the ground, before commencing his meditation: this is further meant to indicate the moment when he becomes centred in his own being and in the universe. He is at the point where heaven and earth are linked by the spear. (Achad, p. 10). The part played by Klingsor is very important in respect to the historical enactment of the symbolic aspect of the music-drama, which we shall touch on later in this chapter. Klingsor wanted to acquire the Grail too, but found that the spear on its own was enough to serve his evil purposes. He represents the *dark* side of human nature, the "unbridled emotions and passions", and the human will acting against divine will.

Spear Symbolism Reinterpreted

Now Hitler's attachment to Wagner's *Parsifal* was obsessive, we are told. The Grail and Spear, Fisher King and the hero Perceval, coming alive before twentieth century audiences, was grist to his mill. He perhaps could not, or did not want to, examine the role of Klingsor! Hitler first beheld the spear in the Hapsburg Treasure House in Vienna in 1909. Resting on its red velvet dais, it was "a solitary spearhead, black with age ... a long tapering point was supported by a wide base with metal flanges depicting the wings of a dove. Within the central aperture of the blade a hammer-headed nail was secured by a cuff threaded with metal wire. On the side of the lowest portion of the base golden crosses were embossed" (Ravenscroft p. 8). The nail, according to one interpretation, symbolized the individual bound by the events of history or his part in the historical process. His freedom depended on the use to which the spear was put, and from the motive that preceded it, presumably a motive arising out of some archetypal energy. The spear itself had this magic, it existed as a concrete object and had supposedly demonstrated its effectiveness in the past. It is sometimes described as the sword of St. Maurice which guarded the tree of life in Eden, or the spear which Paul hurled in anger at

David. During the siege of Antioch at the time of the Crusades, the sudden discovery of the Holy Spear lifted morale, gave the Crusaders strength, and turned what was to be a defeat into victory. It became the possession of the German emperors in the past and became part of the Hapsburg treasure until the 20th century. Only legend links this spear with that of the spear of Longinus or the bleeding lance of Grail Legend. The fact is that, in Hitler's myth, Spear, Grail, and the Perceval story were as inextricably bound as the nail to the blade. On seeing the talisman of power in Vienna for the first time, Hitler felt as if at some earlier period of history he had held the spear himself.

Once established as Dictator, and shortly after his annexation of Austria (1938), he plundered the treasury of the Hapsburgs and took possession of the spear, which was placed in the hall of St. Katherines's in Nuremburg. He thus became the last of a long list of historical figures who once possessed the spear, and were assisted by its "magic" to conquer their enemies in time of crisis. Thus it was the spear of destiny, and the destiny of the world was in his hands. It was ... for a short while! When the Third Reich came tumbling down, the spear fell into the hands of the American occupation forces, and General Eisenhower had it put back in the Hapsburg museum.

Brotherhood of the Grail

Hitler's reconstruction of the Grail myth around the Holy Spear was only part of the story. In the years preceding Hitler's rise to power, his exposure to the Grail myth and other heroic literature, as well as his interest in Wagner's operas, shaped his ideal of a Grail Knight belonging to a Brotherhood of Knights of pure and noble blood, on the adventurous quest of the Holy Spear. He reinterpreted the Christian interpretation of the Grail symbolism to suit his race theory, the Darwinian law of the survival of the fittest in human society, and his "prophetic" vision of the Grail myth as being applicable to events in his own time. The Spear, then, became the starting point of his drive for power, and the Grail Knight of legend the justification for the formation of an *élite,* (the Brotherhood of the Grail). This élite, selected by nature and nurture, would possess all those qualities of loyalty, courage and discipline, to implement his plan for domination and conquest. Hitler was even seen in a photograph showing him dressed in the silvery robe of the Knights of the Grail. We have some words attributed to him, when he was discussing the opera *Parsifal*, which explain his perception of the meaning of the drama. He referred to the strong being concerned with "pure, noble blood, in the protection and glorification of whose purity the Brotherhood of the Initiated have come together ... The King (meaning the Fisher King) is suffering from the incurable disease of corrupted blood" (Sklar, p. 146).

This slanted view was never mentioned by any of the Grail writers. Various explanations are given for the King's state: simply old age, punishment by God, the reaction of a jealous husband for violated honour, taking up arms for an unworthy cause, enchantment in the fairy world, or ineptitude to perform his royal tasks due to the inevitability of rundown and the need for renewal. His affection for Wagner's operas leads one to suggest that here was the spark that started the fire. Wagner's own mystical message is best explained by a monograph written by W. M. Wilmshurst. The character Titurel in *Parsifal*, heard only as a voice in the background, and as the dead Grail King later, we must recognise as the higher self of man. This is "Adam before the Fall into physical conditions, (considering the Fall as a continuous process common to humanity rather than an isolated event occurring to a single being), whilst Amfortas is Adam after it" (p. 14). Amfortas failed as a Grail King because he "allowed one of the hallows — the sacred lance — to become separated from the chalice, and used it for personal ends and desires" (p. 10). To put it another way, in his position as a Grail King, one who is a vessel for divine grace and wisdom, he used his divine life force (the lance) for selfish purposes instead of following Divine Will. Hence, his perpetual suffering and the injunction that he had to "be born again." Parsifal is the third component in this tripartite characterisation. He is the newborn, or regenerated Grail-King-to-be at the end of the drama.

Himmler's Round Table Fellowship

In Hitler's new order, the fusion of the Grail theme with the Round Table tradition was undertaken by Heinrich Himmler, who materialised Hitler's dream, by bringing into existence a Black Brotherhood of Round Table Knights in the twentieth century, with all the notions (barring the Christian, Celtic, or Oriental) associated with the legendary Knights of the Grail. The infamous reputation of this inner clique and their Gestapo is well known. The SS was organised as a secret order within the Nazi Party, topped by an inner circle of twelve, as was Arthur's Table, according to some legends. He attempted to imitate Arthur's court in the castle of Wewelsburg in Westphalia, setting up the Round Table in one of its rooms, with specially designated places for his "knights", and surrounded with appropriate decor. It was completely inaccessible to any but its "guardians", Himmler's élite, who met in secret and meditated on their so-called noble purpose. History has shown that this period of terror and war lasted even less than the short space of Arthurian peace and just rule, certainly less than the projected 1000-year Reich.

The Black Grail

Why did it all happen? Where was the Grail? How can we understand the forces behind the message of the Grail myth? The whole phenomenon, say some who philosophise on the subject, fits into the dualistic doctrine of opposites in the world. If you have a pure (white) Grail, as a symbol of moral purity, then you can also have a black Grail, representing the demoniac powers of the universe. For what the Grail King and his Knights represent, you can also have an anti-Grail King and his Black Knights who are bent on destroying the Kingdom of the Grail. But in the Grail sagas these opposites, for want of a better description, are confronted by Grail heroes, who ultimately find the Grail or fail to do so. Their experience in reconciling these opposites, seen as figures out in the forest, or as energies in the unconscious, will be part of the process of attaining the Grail. All the Grail romances, that is, the stories that contributed to the fashioning of the Grail myth of the Middle Ages, made no reference to the quest for a Black Grail. The "shadow" element in an individual and in the collective leadership of Nazi Germany took control, and translated into thought and action the very opposite of a myth that tried to draw out the best in human nature.

Interpreting Myth

There is a particular character of myth that must be considered here. Given the state of consciousness of any individual or society at any point in time, the energy core of any myth in the unconscious could be expressed in violent or destructive forms. This occurs when the archaic, primitive form of the myth takes on an obsessive character in the psyche of the individual or group. We have experienced as victims, or heard, of "outbursts of evil" from individuals at various times in our lives; at the collective level, where we expect more control, of inhuman acts, violence, aggression, blood sacrifice, scapegoating, which are directed against nations or ethnic groups. We assume that the Grail myth has evolved from its archaic nature, softened by Christian influence and reinterpretation, and presumably integrated into the psyche of modern society; that we have evolved into a higher level of consciousness than our ancestors experienced; and that striking the opposition with fire and sword is a thing of the past. Whitmont described our upward shift in consciousness as having experienced three stages through history. He states that in man's attempt to find meaning in his existence and in his relationships with his fellows and the numinous, he has allowed his consciousness to move from mythological identification to symbolic ritual, from actual slaughter to the Eucharistic mass (where the ritual of transubstantiation is seen as more than symbolic), and is moving further towards interiorization of ritual and myth in the form of psychological meaning for the way we live and function. Mystics and mystical movements (and the Rosicrucians fall into this category) might view this as being applicable to humanity in general. There would be no stages leading from the archaic to the psychological in the mystical community, simply stages of progress on the way to higher consciousness.

Explaining the Hitler Aberration

If we assume Whitmont's three stages as a fair assessment of the development of mankind's development as a species, we can then find a psychological explanation for the phenomenon of Hitler. This is explained as regression, which may occur in individuals and groups in times of rapid transition, when social stability and continuity of traditional values are challenged, when there is a breakdown of law and order, and when individuals or groups cannot adjust to new trends. Repression, rather than sublimation of the "shadow" over centuries, can cause it to break out in most destructive forms. Let us not close our eyes, too, to what has happened in parts of the world since Hitler. At the individual level, Hitler is described as a product of the combined dominance in the ego of the power and demoniac archetypes .

As far as the Grail plays its part in all this, the most definite answer is to be found in John Matthew's work, *The Grail Tradition (9 1,100):* "The Grail is the

Grail is the Grail, and can be nothing else — but there are those who misuse its power, which is neutral like the power of the neutral angels who, according to Wolfram von Eschenbach, first brought the Grail to Earth ... The Grail could be in anybody's care, it could be in ours, but we must learn to use it wisely and demand a level of service which is of the highest kind ... We have to overcome the negative aspects of the Quest within ourselves as well as out there, and thus seeing the dual aspects of the search united in one".

There is no Black Grail, no Brotherhood of Darkness. There is no Grail that throws a shadow, or allows one in, bringing darkness with it. It is so intensely bright that those who are allowed to come close to its centre are forever bathed in light. It is the unity beyond all duality.

Chapter 11

Further Horizons

Proto-Grail in Megalithic Star Temples

While it is certain that the Grail myth was a composite of themes from Celtic, Christian, and Oriental sources, it may also be possible to trace some contribution to an even older source. More than 3500 years before the apostles of Christ celebrated the first Christian mass, using the chalice, wine, and bread as central objects in the Christian mystery, prehistoric people in Europe actually used a prototype of the Grail and performed sacred ceremonies using a stone basin and its contents. At Newgrange and other sites of the Boyne complex in Ireland, Southwestern England, and Brittany, the so-called "passage graves", stone circles, or "star temples" supply evidence of this. These huge stone structures were built by tribal communities at sacred locations where earth and stellar energies were strong, in which advanced mathematics, sacred geometry and astronomy were used to site and orient their temples. The architectural plan of these mounds and circles, their geomantic and mathematical siting, the objects used in their ceremonies, the symbolic messages left in stone, and other remains hint at a belief (or knowledge?) that "heaven and earth were connected at certain locations marked by underground water systems which acted in a spiral fashion" (Harrison, p.19). It is conceivable that these early temple builders knew intuitively, if not by reflection, that harmonious relationships among living creatures depended upon certain harmonies established with the earth and with physical forces. The sacred structures and the rites performed in and about them, were a means of bringing people's questing spirit into attunement with subliminal natural forces and the cosmos. The temple became the point of entry into what was described much later as the Otherworld of the Celts, and in the Grail romances, the castle of the Grail.

Earliest Models of Grail Temple

No great feat of the imagination would be required to visualise the kind of rituals performed there and to conclude that these great monuments were the earliest models of the Grail castle or temple. The whole tumulus at Newgrange suggests a use above that of mere burial. Its shape as a pregnant part of the surface of the Earth Mother, suggestive of fertility, creativity and life, with a long passage access to and from the interior of the womb, shows a concern with the mystery of life and death. The etched spiral design on the huge entrance stone which is again repeated on one of the tall side stones of the wall of the passage towards the central chamber, symbolises the three degrees in the initiatory journey of the soul, the rites of passage of each neophyte into the mysteries of this particular cult. The ritual that effected the spiritual transformation of each candidate must have been heightened by the structure of the place, the objects, and symbols which were part of his experience and instruction. The central chamber with its corbelled ceiling of rocky plates rises to a height of twenty feet (the heart of the Grail castle), with three niches on the sides and around the circular chamber; the astronomical orientation of the passage to allow a shaft of light from the sun at the winter solstice to enter the central chamber; the ritual objects, including the stone basin or proto-Grail, and the mysterious symbols on the walls of the central chamber, must have all been the components of an initiation ceremony enacting a myth of creation involving a solar god and an earth goddess in which the prospective initiate was the main participant.

Newgrange, Knowth, and Dowth, located within a short distance of each other would have been part of a great initiatory complex, having all the physical and spiritual conditions that would contribute to the instruction and experience serving the needs of a public cult participating in the *lesser mysteries,* and a smaller private group, whose membership would be determined by spiritual worthiness or readiness to receive exposure to the higher mysteries of life. We could equate the latter with the Grail knights of medieval legend. Peregrinations to, and between the great mounds at specific times of the year, related to the movements of the sun, an assembly perhaps at the large mounded circle (about the size of a football oval), the final arrival at the Newgrange tumulus, the entry into the long passage dimly lit by torches, the awesome darkness and stillness when the torches were extinguished, the sudden exposure to "earth currents" concentrated in the area, the flooding of the chamber by a shaft of light from the sun during the mid-winter solstice, and the final revelation of the Grail and its contents, would find its equivalent in the knight's quest in the wilderness, his experiences with the unknown, and his reception into the Grail castle. The culminating point or the final initiation, in the one case, would be the experience and revelation following the entry of sunlight into the dark inner chamber, the focal point of the meeting of earth and solar energies, and in the other case, the illuminating Grail experience and elevation of the questing knight to Grail kingship.

Knight's Quest Like Shamanic Journey

The religious culture which inspired the building of these monuments is believed to have been shamanic directed. The rituals for an inner shamanic caste would mirror the experiences of the shaman. It is here that comparisons may be made with the Knight's quest, which would approximate the shaman's dream sequence of separation and return, of challenging encounters on the journey, and of reaching a state of trance or ecstasy. One becomes a shaman by "being called"; Perceval was first called by the Grail when he met a group of Arthur's knights in their shinning armour with caparisoned horses, weaponry, pennants and other trappings, and he mistook them for angels. This encounter with masculinity in all its splendour stirred him deeply and provided the stimulus to break away from his mother and seek Arthur's court. That he possessed in potential the shamanic gift or magic and the power to overcome, derived from the ancestral connection of every shaman, we are told later in the story and also in his initial successes against other knights.

There is also the strange episode where Perceval is transfixed by some spots of blood on the snow, left by a wounded swan. He has difficulty pulling out of this trance-like state until Gawain finds a way to restore him to normal consciousness. Again, the hermit Trevrizent plays a part not unlike that of a master shaman in Perceval's development as the healer-hero; he communicated certain spiritual truths and miraculous powers to Perceval after he had completed his passage through the "*dark night*" and "*crossed the threshold*" of final initiation into the higher mysteries. Trevrizent was also related to the Grail King, as was Perceval. All of which suggests that Perceval was being gradually inducted into an exclusive caste of Grail Guardianship. It is well known that the shaman undergoes a mental crisis, which cuts him off from tribal life for a while; this happened to Perceval when he was cut off from the community of the Grail Kingdom after his failure to live up to expectations on his first visit. The period of crisis, and his survival after the experience, is itself proof of the prospective shaman's *"initiation"*, of passing the test; since he receives his power because of the experience of crisis. This is the beginning of a sudden *"hierophantic realisation"* which places him above his tribe in matters of the spirit. It is in this state that Perceval is able to use his power as healer and assume the status of Grail King.

A Golden Age

One could hypothesise, as we read the symbols in and about the mound, and note the solar orientation of the star temple, that the main thrust of any winter dawn ceremony was to impress upon the initiate how the Solar God would meet the Earth Mother, in love, and together re-enact the cycle of creation. Perhaps the society that started these rituals which focussed on the intimacy of heaven, earth and human life, were in possession of certain of life's secrets, where male and female principles were in balance in the human psyche, and these in turn contributed to social harmony. If this were so, then the Golden Age was a historical fact rather than a nostalgic dream.

Jessie Weston's Hypothesis

There is a perspective of the Grail myth which makes it a literary record of age-old vegetation ritual, a ritual based on a persistence of these ancient beliefs in Medieval Europe. The availability of historical and mythological evidence closer to our time gives greater credibility to this view than the reconstruction offered above of the rituals of prehistoric man. Views vary as to whether myth preceded ritual or vice versa, but the hypothesis advanced here is that the Grail myth followed an actual ritual; that is, the Grail romances were not imaginative creations of the Grail poets, but a literary record of rituals practised by the successors of the ancient oriental mystery cults.

Several writers have advanced this view in general terms, but it was Jessie Weston who boldly made it central to the understanding of the diverse elements in the Grail myth, presenting a lot of evidence and argument in support of it. Her insights have been accepted enthusiastically by some scholars, and by others, with a great deal of scepticism, possibly because it played down other interpretations. Her arguments are well worth setting out here. She asserts that the ancient vegetation cults had evolved to a point where the mystery had a double intent in order to serve two types of participant in the mystery religion. Where the intent was *exoteric,* the ceremony was open to the whole community, and it confined its revelation to that of the "lesser mysteries". When *esoteric,* it was a revelation to a few who could apprehend the "greater mysteries." The greater mysteries had doctrinal or wisdom value and culminated in a noetic experience. This was more than the understanding and satisfaction gained in the more public or lesser mystery, which imparted a basic knowledge about the link between mankind, nature, and the supernatural, and was motivated by the attempt to influence events by magic.

Finding it difficult to accept explanations given on the origins and import of the Grail myth, and the inner coherence of the symbols, persons, and events of the Quest, she has pointed to the rituals of widespread vegetation cults in ancient Babylon, Phrygia, Greece, Europe of the Middle Ages, and even in contemporary tribal societies, as the original base of the myth. Even the Christian mystery is recognised as incorporating transposed elements of these pre-Christian mystery cults. In their evolved state the cults used their ritual to communicate an understanding of the purposes and processes of Creation and the reconstitution of Life on a cosmic scale. As Weston would say it:

"*These cults were considered not only the most potent factors for assuring the material prosperity of the land and folk, but were also held to be the most appropriate vehicle for imparting the highest religious teaching ... While the material end was the sole one sought by the masses, the non-material one was sought in addition, rather than instead, by the elite*". (xxxii—xxxiv)

Mithraic Mysteries

The link between these ancient mystery cults and the practitioners of the secret tradition in Europe of the Middle Ages which found expression in Grail literature, were the groups in the twelfth and thirteenth centuries whose doctrines and ritual pointed to their Manichaeistic, Gnostic, or Mithraic origin. We know much about Mithraic doctrine and ritual. Descriptions of the nature of Mithraic ritual always refer to the seven degrees of initiation, designated by human and animal symbols to represent respectively the roles or attributes of each. Each degree indicates the particular level of progress of the Mithraic initiate to the "region of the stars" or the highest level of consciousness. In order of progression they were the raven, the magician, the warrior, the lion, the Persian, the sun, and the father. Mithraism, before Christianity became the official religion of the declining Roman Empire, was embraced by Roman soldiery and thus spread into the farthest limits of the Roman occupation of Europe, as the legions moved from one frontier to another.

Mithraism was not eliminated by the state religion, but continued to survive in secret in the late Middle Ages. Manly Hall believes that the Catharistic reference to seven transmigrations being required to "*attain the Light*", probably referred to quasi-Mithraic seven degrees of initiation to achieve the status of *Perfectus*. But Ravenscroft sees an exact parallel, apart from the changes in the symbolism during the Middle Ages, in the degrees of progress of the Mithraic initiate and the experiences of the knight in quest of the Grail. One may easily note the similarities in name of some of the degrees, for example, warrior becomes knight, the magician becomes mentor or hermit, the Grail replaces the sun, the Grail King is a father figure, the pelican, eagle, swan, and peacock substitute for the raven, lions or other animals represent other challenging psychic experiences. In the one case, the place of mystical transformation was within the temple, in the other, in the world of nature, society, and in the otherworld.

Cathar Rites

Aside from this interpretation, there is some evidence of the use of graded instruction and status among the Cathars. The first stage of spiritual progress was induction into the *Tradition*. This was intended to prepare and sustain the *Credentes* or Believers, from whom a less strenuous discipline was demanded. They lived the faith as best they could in anticipation of advancement or as simple and contented devotees. The *Perfecti* were those who extirpated sensual desire from their lives, who were vegetarian, remained celibate, and whose souls had attained a high degree of "purity". We are reminded here of the tendency of the Grail writers to describe their Grail Maiden as "pure", and the designation by Wolfram von Eschenbach of his Grail Knights as being the purest. The Cathar *Perfecti* participated in the *consolamentum* rite, which prepared them for the sacrifices they had to make and consoled them for the trials they had to face in accepting their new status. One of the most touching examples that history provides of spiritual courage is the decision made by some Credentes and Knights who, the evening before the Cathar defenders of Montségur resolved to surrender to the forces that besieged them, to partake of the consolamentum rite. In doing so they well knew the consequences of this commitment, and on the next day they willingly threw themselves into the punitory fires that awaited them. At some point the Cathars would also share a sacramental meal associated with the *manisola* rite. The time for this was linked with the sun's orientation at Montségur. The light of the sun coming through a window in a wall at a certain time of the year could resemble the Grail entering the Grail Castle of romance and spiritually nourishing all the Knights of the Round Table.

Add this knowledge to what legend tells us about the Magdalenian Grail being in the care of this gnostic sect, and you have among the Cathar *Perfecti* those who were eminently suitable to serve the Grail as its Guardians. When we also recall that the troubadours, the bards of Europe, had their origins in the South of France, and that women like Esclarmonde de Foix were also Cathar Perfecti, we have a mix which connects Grail, Grail Castle, and Grail Guardians — the noble and otherworldly stuff of the Grail romances — with actual people promoting a tradition that in many ways ran counter to religious orthodoxy and who ultimately suffered the consequences of their "heresy".

Templar Initiates

The third recognisable movement that fitted into this secret tradition were the Templars. That they had their secret ceremonies to which only certain Templars were admitted is a fact. To find out what these were in form or content was made a fruitless endeavour by the Inquisition. Hence what the Templars practised in private remains a mystery. Much is made of the secret object or idol called *Baphomet:* speculation as to what it was ranges from the shroud of Jesus, to a human head or something demoniac or monstrous. It is possible that the Templar initiates, because of their intimate contact with knightly orders of Islam and the survivals of mystery teaching and of mental alchemy in the Middle East, may have developed rites that were a blend of the western and eastern mystery traditions.

What is common to these three movements — Mithraic, Cathar and Templar —was also their practice of having sacred objects revealed to their initiates at some crucial point in their initiatory rites. Modern esoteric and lodge-based brotherhoods have perpetuated this practice in accordance with their claims of descent in the Great Tradition. At the time of the writing of the Grail romances, the survivors of the Mithraic cult would have continued the custom of revealing to their advanced neophytes a statue or relief of a lion-headed figure, encoiled by a Serpent, at some advanced point in the ritual designed to achieve an inner transformation. The physical display accompanied by sound and light effects would both awe and instruct the candidate as its message was grasped. The Cathars, likewise were presumed to have a Grail or some treasure of spiritual value, or some special knowledge which the *perfecti* possessed. It could have been simply the apprehension gained by a candidate for initiation, after he or she had been duly prepared, that the Holy Spirit within him or her was no longer bound by the chains of the flesh. In the case of the Templars, the view has been expressed that *Baphomet* may have been a human head, which in Celtic tradition had great spiritual value. We may be reminded here of the Welsh story of Perceval, the *Peredur,* which has a Grail Castle visit in which the Grail appears as the head of a decapitated human. The head of the Celtic god-hero Bran kept his warriors entertained for quite some time before it was buried in London facing the Continent to protect Britain from future invasions. Whatever the object or idea was in the mysteries that lay in the background of the Grail romances, its revelation to initiates was calculated to inspire and awe, and also to reward. The object or symbol must have in addition carried immense personal empowerment — as evidenced by the exemplary character of the Templars as Knights of the Cross. We may concede this, despite some reports about some members of the Order falling short of their high ideals of chivalry.

To all this we may add the reference made in an earlier chapter to the romance of *Perlesvaus,* in which the Grail is described in shifting manifestations. Though four of the forms of the Grail (a child, a wounded and suffering man, a crowned king, and a chalice) could have referred to the Christian mystery and the chalice as the Grail, the fifth was an indescribable (dreadful?) manifestation. Why couldn't it have been described? Could the anonymous writer, whom one presumes to have had Templar associations, have been presenting some information only to those who understood? Were those who understood in contact with initiates of some threatened unorthodox mystery cult, or were they in fact initiates themselves?

These Grail objects were venerated and revealed only to the highest initiates of these movements. Scholars disagree about the extent to which the Grail romances actually recorded the practices of secret mystery cults or were simply a literary outpouring of the prevailing mood of dissent from Church doctrine. The evidence presented above strongly suggests that the Grail romances were a cryptic record of secret rituals.

"Lesser" and "Higher" Mysteries

Such a perspective of mystery religion and the survival of its aspirations and rituals among mystic groups at the time of the flowering of the Grail romances finds accord with a Rosicrucian understanding of this aspect of the Great Tradition that has existed alongside, and sometimes within, the orthodox, mainstream or state religion. Assuming that the induction into the *lesser* mysteries prepared novitiates for their ascent into the *higher,* they would be expected to acquire some knowledge of their own nature, their place and function in, and their obligations to, society. Their character would reflect some basic morality and ethics, and an understanding of life and life's processes. They would also acquire a thirst to pursue worthy aims in life, based on self-knowledge. One could say that all the experiences of a knight like Perceval that occurred outside the Grail Kingdom were of this nature. The impact of these encounters in the mundane world on one's own transformation has been dealt with in some detail in the chapter on "Symbols and Archetypes of the Grail Quest."

Now the *higher* mysteries would include those phases where Perceval lived through his past experiences and received the blessing of the hermit Trevrizent, followed by his second admittance to the Grail castle and the final initiation, where he becomes the healer and takes the place of the father figure, the Grail King. At this stage, the knight's elevation is analogous to the revelations received by higher initiates into the mysteries. These revelations would relate to a more profound knowledge of the mysteries of birth, death, and resurrection, and the intimate relationship of humanity with nature and the cosmos. It is this meaning that has to be extracted from Perceval's experiences in the other world castle of the Grail, the ritual in the banquet hall, the strange circumstances of the Fisher King and the Wasteland, the symbols and messages imparted during the banquet where he witnesses the Grail Procession, and Perceval's first failure and later success in that theatre of initiation. Since, in the mystery rites, no revelation was made public of the final initiatory act, and only in a coded form in the imagery of the Grail romances, we must assume that there was a revelation of the secret gnosis or truths about what the mystery school tradition wished to communicate. The best we can say of the purpose of the mystery initiation is expressed by Ravenscroft: "Their purpose was to create a temporary dissociation from physical sense—awareness in order to enter higher realms of consciousness and time through which the fullness of the spiritual world was made manifest" (p. 30)

If we return to the subject of Weston's thesis, we find her offering a list of parallels between the content of the Grail romances and the specific practices found in the various mystery religions. There is the common sacramental meal in the banquet in which specific vessels play a part; in some mysteries the celebrants drank or ate from the vessels, and in the Grail banquet the Grail becomes the most important object, which mysteriously provides the food of life; the candidate's tests and trials in the older mysteries were the personal enactment of the death and revival of the god, while in the Fisher King's ritual, the King, as representative of the god, was healed by the hero (noting here that the king and hero were two aspects of the same personality), the Grail and Lance as fertility symbols, transformed into a higher spiritual concept, became elements of symbolic meaning in the understanding of the Eucharist; and finally, there is the Grail King/ Wasteland nexus. All these have their parallels in the Attis/Adonis, the Phrygian, and other Oriental mysteries (147—8). Additionally, we find support for her thesis in postulating the presence of a link between the Grail Maiden bearing a vessel with the unlimited capacity to nourish people magically; and with the importance given to the Mother Goddess holding a bowl in a position under her breasts, suggestive of the idea of her eternal milk-bearing character to maintain the life that is born. Michael Dames even finds a thread of connection between the Silbury Hill mystery and the Fisher King of the Grail Legend. If we view the base plan of this monument (which is that of a squatting female) from the east, he tells us: "the male element appears between the breast and knee, in the phallic shape of the inter causeway moat. In this context ... every mother goddess had a male consort (ultimately part of her own body) whose energy, sexual wounding, and annual death played a vital role in the birth process. This pattern is reflected in the wounded Fisher King of the Medieval Grail legend ..." (p. 80)

Celtic Cauldron and the Otherworld

Some research explores in great detail the Celtic contributions to the shaping of the Grail myth without lining up to confirm Weston's "from ritual to romance" hypothesis. However, in respect to the ritual of the mystery school tradition as it emerged in the west and not the east, one does not have to look further than the myth of Keridwen's cauldron and its ritualistic base in the Druidic mysteries.

The myth of Keridwen is an allegorical representation of a ritual drama used to impress upon the novitiate the cycle of birth, necessity, death and the rebirth of the *new man*. The theme of the initiate's escape from the womb (Gwion from his stewardship, and Perceval from his mother's influence), the changes in form of Gwion and the Goddess (the various stages of the initiate and the changes in character of the priestess), the persistence of a female figure throughout the hunt for Gwion, and female figures in the Perceval quest (the moderating influence of the feminine principle); the final swallowing of Gwion by Keridwen in the form of a grain of wheat by the hen Keridwen, and Gwion's final second rebirth from Keridwen's womb (the spiritual rebirth of Perceval of the Healing of the wound of the Grail King and the Wasteland) — the similarities are evident though the metaphors appear different. Gwion was in flight from the Mother Goddess and was eventually captured, and Perceval's journey was prompted by an inner urge, but both myths presented the theme of separation and return. Other similarities in detail are noticeable. The Gwion adventure starts with three drops of magic fluid "accidentally" falling onto the hand of the hero. This is not unlike the drops of blood falling onto the hand of the young spear-bearer in the Grail Procession. Gwion tastes the magic fluid, while Perceval enters a trance when he sees the drops of swan's blood in the snow.

The Descent to Annwn

The Celtic fount provides further food for the Grail story. If we look at Bardic literature, we find the story of Arthur's descent to Annwn to save a friend and capture a magic cauldron. This would have provided some of the framework for the later Grail quest. One can also transpose Perceval's journey into the Bardic three levels of progress. Perceval's quest is akin to the soul's journey in three circles of existence (Abred, Gwynvydd, and Ceugant) in Celtic mythology. Abred is the circle of crude experience, of ignorance and misconduct. This corresponds broadly to Perceval as a Fool and all those experiences leading up to his visit to the Grail castle; Gwynvydd, where he enjoys some freedom from Abred, and a temporary moment of bliss; the failure on the question test causes an arrest or an apparent regression when he enters into a period of despair, finally, his ascent into Gwynvydd, where he remains as Grail King, in the Celtic circle of happiness. It took a later Christian version of the Grail myth to include the circle of Ceugant where Galahad was hero. He was absorbed into the heaven, the All, which to the Bard was Ceugant, where God resides.

We note here that whereas the ritualised myths of old were celebrated as a ceremony or ceremonies in chosen locations where the participant went through the processes, vicariously, of the events in the life of the god of their respective cult, this had to be enacted differently in the literary medium. All the events were *"externalised"* in the journey of the hero. The magic of the Grail myth was presented to the listener by the troubadour orally or offered in writing by the Grail poet, but the instrument of transfer of the initiatic message was the receiver's imagination and capacity to empathise. The novitiate (the one who heard the story) was outside the scene, but was able to internalise the sequence of events and was personally transformed by the unfolding drama.

Exile and Return

The question of a Golden Age being an imaginative construct or an actuality, has also broadened the area of discussion on the enigma of the Grail myth. This Golden Age has been described by some scholars as projection by angst-ridden people of an ideal world, which may or may not have existed in actuality. One may also describe it as a vision of a lost paradise springing from the human heart and mankind's effort to find a lost relationship with a Supreme Being. This feeling of loss is generally explained in terms of moral delinquency or unworthiness.

In this view, the Grail myth is a picture of this separation of mankind from its ideal condition, its awareness of its fallen state, and its attempt to return to paradise. Caitlin Matthews, in her beautiful essay on Sophia, suggests that the Grail is a cup of wisdom and compassion, standing for the gnostic *Sophia* and the Kabbalistic *shekinah,* both being personified, and both being present in mankind, alleviating regret for the fall and feeding the dream to return to mankind's original state. The way mankind is behaving right now reveals that we are in exile. 'We are," she says, "in a state of forgetfulness. We have lost ... our state of union with the divine ... The Wasteland is our state of exile: the place that is not paradise ... The Grail is that piece of paradise which remains among us, hidden and transcendent, the cup of sovereignty, of wisdom: a draft of that cup is a remembrance of paradise, a union of soul with God. The Wounded King is the potential Grail Knight himself, a symbol of lost sovereignty ..." (p. 124). Sophia, the holy wisdom of God accompanies the Grail seeker, though he may be unaware of it; yet it exercises a powerful energy as a motivator.

Erich Fromm, the psychologist, holds a similar thought though not in a cosmic context, when he explains his concept of the individual's "escape from freedom": individuals escape from control by parents or primary social groups in their earlier years; this produces a sense of isolation and separateness; they then spend the rest of their lives trying to escape from this freedom by seeking personal identity in society and in the world about them. Louis-Claude de Saint Martin, the 18th century mystic, uses a succinct image to describe the human condition: "we are in a widowed state and we seek to remarry."

Many ancient myths talk of mankind falling out of harmony with God; religion and ritual tries to lead the way back to a restoration of this harmony. This was indeed the lament of the Wounded King and of his retainers and subjects who attended the banquet of the Grail castle; hence their enormous plaint when Perceval failed to ask the question on his first visit. The enchantment of the Grail King, his unhappy people, and barren land, is this condition of exile. The Grail King healed by the fully matured Perceval and the disenchantment of the Wasteland is the return to paradise.

The myth of the Grail quest endures amongst us. It is becoming more prominent in the human consciousness today, because its message is trying to break through the ego's censor of the unconscious, as it has done at various time in the past. The integration of the myth into the life of the conscious ego calls us to re-direct our goals in a new quest, and take us beyond the desperate hope that paradise would somehow be given to us by the intervention of some mysterious force, to that of actualising or realising this beatific state by mankind's collective effort. How shall we recover our lost happiness? "First of all," says Caitlin Matthews, "by assuming a sense of responsibility towards ourselves; this is not selfishness but common sense. Only those who start the journey deserve to win the Grail; if we wait for anyone else to 'join our party we shall never begin. It does not matter if we make mistakes along the way…" To which we add: while we undertake the journey individually, we know that we are not alone; all the other knights of the Round Table have entered the forest, at different points of entry, on the journey home, but none held back from the test.

Celtic Cross, author's photo.

Chapter 12

Psychological and Mystical Perspectives

In this final chapter on the Grail and Grail Quest, we must synthesise, or at least coordinate, the various perspectives presented in this challenging myth. It was mentioned earlier that, as mankind's consciousness has evolved to a higher level, we have tended "to memorise ritual and myth in the form of psychological meaning for the way we live and function" (Whitmont, p.166). We have sought to find, in the fields of analytical, humanistic and transpersonal psychology, a meaningful framework for a better understanding of the myth and its application as a didactic arid inspirational resource in our lives. Our survey of the Grail legend and secondary literature made us touch on the structure and dynamics of the psyche, the conscious and unconscious mind, the personal and collective unconscious, the main archetypes and images of the unconscious, and the process of individuation, or integration, or self-actualisation, in order to grasp the message of the myth.

Archetype of the Self

Fundamental to understanding the secret of the Grail Quest is the importance given, in the psychological explanation, to the archetype of the self. This archetype represents mankind's striving for unity, and has the overarching role of holding together all the archetypes and systems of the psyche. Yet as we live our daily lives, its full potential is not "actualised"; that is, the self remains "entrapped" during a long period of human growth and development in interaction with the environment. But awareness of this power within our psyche must cause us to wonder at our reluctance to constantly use it. The self is both the agent and the goal of the process of individuation. It is the activator, and the final reward. The self is the Grail companion, the hidden and neglected motivator, the potential healer of the "wounded" immature psyche, and it is also the final illuminator or reintegrator. In spiritual terms, the self has to be "redeemed" from the darkness of that aspect of human nature, or the darkness of the unconscious; therefore, the rational ego has to be "crucified" or "sacrificed" to redeem the self. The language may be a bit severe here, it is the language of the mystics. The psychologist does not see the ego as being sacrificed. Rather, it sees its quality being enhanced or its nature changed, in the transformation process that eventually makes the ego responsive at all times to the harmonising impulses of the self. The myth tells us that this takes will, effort and testing experience or suffering. The hierophants of the ancient mysteries knew the secrets of transformation and used their knowledge and skills to facilitate or accelerate an initiate's progress. The Grail troubadours of the Middle Ages knew these secrets; they concealed their unorthodox spiritual truths in song and fable to avoid persecution. The mental alchemists knew these — they revealed their technique of spiritual alchemy to their initiates only through the metaphors of the transmutation of metals, and in symbolic pictorial representations and verse. In its various forms the Great Tradition has continued to the present, with reduced secrecy due to the steady movement towards toleration.

Journey of the Ego

To reiterate, then, Perceval's quest may be seen as the journey of the ego, prompted initially by the self, going through all its adventures, forced into colloquy with all the elements of the unconscious, harnessing and coordinating its archetypal energies of the unconscious, aided by the archetypes of the self, often through its mediator, the anima. By reconciling the opposites in his psyche, through recognition and acceptance of their place in his life and coming to terms with them, he has a true experience of his real self; as expressed in the metaphor of the legend, he enters the Grail castle for the second time and knows what to do. Since the centre of gravity shifts to the true centre of his being he becomes the healer of wounds, the restorer of fertility and happiness to the Kingdom and its King. He has integrated the unconscious elements of his psyche into his conscious life. When we consider the sub-myth of the Wounded Fisher King and the Wasteland, we are exposed to the nature of the collective psyche, and the place of the individual in it. The happy conclusion to the myth (the healing of King and Land) reinforces our obligation to care for the earth and our environment. The law of cause and effect applies both at the individual and the collective level, and the collective is both the sum and product of its individual components.

But all things start with the individual. If society is too slow to accelerate the movement towards raising its level of consciousness, to avert the threat to the survival of our species, and to understand its place in the cosmos, those who know the answers, who are the prophets, who are the individuated or integrated, must show the way. This is the greatest obligation of the hero, the true mystic. As Marsha Sinetar said: "the inception of real personality health occurs when an individual stops trying to get the world to meet their needs and wants, and begins seeking out ways to perform some needed and meaningful service for others" (p.3). Those who have nearly completed the Quest will know what to do and how to act. But there are many who may accept Sinetar's advice as rational and sensible, yet are unable to act. The Grail castle vanishes before them, and they must submit to the further tests of experience, and the rational, conscious ego must lift its censor on the unconscious and commence the process of transformation.

The psychologist views their human subjects as mentally (psychically) healthy or unhealthy, emotionally disturbed or balanced, temperamentally unsound or stable, dependent or autonomous, impulsive or hesitant, violent or pacific, brash or tender, ego-oriented or self-oriented, and many other designations to describe a person's state or his or her behavioural responses. The final state of integration or wholeness is delimited as a degree of mental health that is achieved often by means of an inner struggle of an individual to resolve the splits or opposites within his or her psyche. One could approximate this, in mythological terms, to the end of the quest, the final vision of, or reception into the Grail.

Self-Actualisation

Abraham Maslow, the humanistic psychologist, worked on a similar concept to Carl Jung's process of individuation. He based his progress of human development on the satisfaction of needs, the end point being that of self-actualisation. In his model, human beings proceed up a pyramid of needs, from the time of their birth and through their life time. They are motivated first by safety and survival needs, the psychological needs, and later intellectual and creative needs and interests. The final need after all the other needs have been satisfied, though not necessarily in a rigid hierarchical pattern, is the need to find self-fulfilment and realise one's full potential, or the need to actualise self. Using scientific method, gathering and recording data from college students and others, and forming hypotheses, Maslow finally described his self-actualisers as having certain distinguishing characteristics. Some of these include: seeing things as they really are; not being upset by uncertainties; behaving spontaneously and showing no anxiety or guilt, hence being free of neurotic symptoms; having a good sense of humour, being creative, and making good use of their talents and abilities; being generally concerned with the welfare of mankind; understanding and experiencing the basic experiences in life; being less influenced by the social environment; and possessing values of beauty, goodness and truth.

Now the terms "individuated" or "actualised" would naturally convey an idea of finality, of no further development. And this has been criticised on the philosophical ground that "everything is becoming" and nothing stays the same. Maslow did not postulate a finished "type", but a general configuration of attitudinal and character traits to be found to predominate among those who proceeded beyond the level of creative needs and interests. Maslow also noted that his self-actualisers had what he called "peak" experiences, moments of happiness and fulfillment — a sort of momentary glimpse of illumination. We can compare this with having a first vision of the Grail, when it sees fit to present itself to us as it did quite suddenly at the Round Table. We may be inclined to equate Maslow's point of self -actualisation as the moment when Perceval solves his own problem of identity, solves the problem of the Grail King and his kingdom, and attains Grail Kingship. But wait ...

In the later years, Maslow's further observations of people who were even "superior" to those who reached the top of the hierarchy of needs and interests, strained the validity of his hypothesis. There were further dimensions to human nature. Some people were seen to go beyond self-actualisation and to function on a transcendental and transpersonal level. They enjoyed "extreme health", not merely that of psychic comfort or consciousness, and went beyond ego boundaries and the limitations of space and time. They were people who transcended self.

This posed problems of classification, which could only be done on the reports of such "superior" people once they could be identified. As well, objective verification could only be achieved if the investigators had the same experiences as were reported. The broad class identified included mystics, meditators, exponents of Buddhist psychology, yogis, persons who experienced high levels of consciousness and whose experiences were described in such terms as illumination, enlightenment, annihilation, liberation, cosmic consciousness, or union with God. Psychologists in general have avoided the area, which only students of mystical and religious experiences have tried to describe with great difficulty. The newer field of transpersonal psychology has taken up the challenge, and models are being worked out. In whatever way the state of illumination or its generic associates convey, whether the state is a temporary phenomenon (for example "seeing the Grail") or a more permanent transformation (Buddhahood, or Christ consciousness, "being the Grail" or "drinking its contents"), the meaning of the self is seen in a wider context. It is not merely the centre of individual consciousness, but is part of the *Greater Self*, analogous to what the mystics have variously called the Oversoul, the Universal Mind, Brahman, Tao, or Cosmic Consciousness. Maslow later described this state of Being as that which went beyond the reach of experience of his self-actualised person. It is the state achieved when the individual becomes "transpersonal, transhuman, centred in the cosmos, rather than in human needs and interest, going beyond humanness, identity, self-actualisation, and the like".

This view of self will be in accord with what the Rosicrucians, having studied the reports of mystics and philosophers, and the truths contained in mythology, have taught for centuries. The Rosicrucian regards the self as a manifestation of the cosmic in all its glory, a reflection of the Cosmic Mind. The point of absorption between what was initially seen by the individual to be separate from what was part of a Supreme reality is described as the ultimate mystical experience. It is the unknown, open-ended part of Ken Wilber's "spectrum of consciousness" where "the Self/Not-Self boundary breaks at the transpersonal bands and vanishes into the level of Mind" (p. 75). In the context of the Grail mystery, it could be likened to the drinking of the contents of the Grail by the Grail Knight, or becoming the Grail, where the level of consciousness reached by the individual sees no differentiation between what he observes and the object of his observation, where reality is experienced as non-dual or One.

Three Knights who Attained the Grail

There were three knights in one of the Grail stories who had Grail experiences above that of the other knights of the Round Table, namely, Galahad, Perceval, and Bors. They took the Grail in Solomon's boat to Sarras, presumed to be Jerusalem. With them was Perceval's sister, who was with them for part of the journey. She was the human image of the Grail, who gave her life by giving her own blood to save another. The whole drama of selfless love and compassion, of creation, of sacrifice, nourishment and renewal are enacted here. This is the Grail as most of us can understand it. On reaching Sarras, Galahad followed the Grail into heaven, rising beyond the peak of illumination in this world. Perceval, now downgraded because of the Christian emphasis on a more ascetic hero figure like Galahad, stays behind as the Grail King, enjoying that beatific state in this world. Bors returned to Arthur's court to tell the tale. He was the gift of the Grail to struggling humanity, to the Lancelots and the Gawains who failed in the quest through human frailty, but whose hopes never die. We may be able to place these three knights, in a limited way, in three categories of the scale of Being, within the perspective of humanistic and transpersonal psychology. Galahad went beyond the boundaries of ego and was absorbed into the cosmic, vanishing into the level of Mind. Perceval remained at a heightened level of consciousness, short of complete absorption. Bors went once more among those who saw no further vision of the Grail, moving up and down the "spectrum of consciousness", a constant example and inspiration to those wanting reassurance that the pursuit of the practical and the sacred could, if joined together, make the worthwhile life, of those who would one day see the Grail.

The Western Mystical Approach

The allegory of the Knight on the mystic quest characterises the Western mystical approach to transcendence. The quest must be an active one, prompted by the drive toward integration, or self-realisation, or reintegration with divinity. It must be strengthened by the will, sustained by persistence, softened by the heart, deriving its experiences from interaction with nature and with human society, focussed on a belief in something greater that the quester, and a nostalgic dream to reach for a spiritual nobility that is the seeker's birthright. Static contemplation or reflection does play an important part, but only as rest and revitalising points on the difficult journey. It is a journey full of disappointments and setbacks, contrasting with feelings of hope and moments of triumph. But success is assured to the courageous, the patient, the persevering. A process of steady purification occurs with the struggle; and if necessary, help is at hand ... help from the Grail, which is after all hidden within us. Today's students on the mystical path, make the journey of the Grail hero. They follow a path of initiation that has been tracked by adepts of the ancient mystery schools. In pursuing this Journey, unwavering in their resolve to complete the quest, mystical students can condense "many lifetime's experiences into one, and absorb the understanding that such experiences bring into a shorter span of time" (Ashcroft—Nowicki, p. 198). As knight-mystics, they start the journey as innocent Fools, but finally attain the Guardianship of the Grail, the highest order of chivalry, the phase of enlightenment, of cosmic consciousness; they are born to a new life.

While Arthur and his knights were banqueting at their Round Table one day, a stupefying event occurred that indirectly heralded the decline and fall of the Fellowship of the Round Table, the death of the King, and the return to barbarism, which ended the temporary paradise created by Arthur's rule. The event, paradoxically, was the visit of the Grail. It floated into the hall in a blaze of light, placed itself at the centre of the Table, proceeded to nourish all who were present, and then floated away. Gawain jumped up from his seat and committed himself to search for the Grail. Others followed his example, and pursued their individual quests. The spiritual archetype of the Round Table Fellowship had manifested on the mundane plane and had run its course, the price paid for human error. But the cycle was started again, as if the new egg was incubating in the collapsing state of the Fellowship. Honoured as the best knights in the kingdom, the Fellowship was given the spiritual nourishment by the Grail that the new quest may be started, a Fellowship that was being rewarded for having tried to make the noblest aspirations of chivalry actualise heaven on earth. From the moment of the Grail's brief visit, the fortunes of each knight were left to move him to the next level of initiation.

The Grail search was to be an individual journey in which initiative, personal will, and ardent desire to seek final initiation as knights of the Grail. But within each knight was the memory of the Round Table Fellowship. Each left the Table with the thought firmly imprinted in his consciousness that he was on the quest not only for himself, but for his order of chivalry whose aim was to serve humanity, for those whose time had not yet come, for those who have not yet heard the call, or seen the distant light, of the Grail. Each knight-mystic of today knows in their heart that after the quest is over, they will remain as a beacon to those who hear their tale. They will return like Bors, who became the avatar, one who has "been there", wanting to share their wisdom with those who are still on the quest, and with those yet to start. It is in this way that they serve the Grail, as the Grail served them once, and they must reflect its spirit among their human companions. From this group will arise the vision and the power to create the next Round Table, one that will correspond in all its parts to the heavenly one above.

Glastonbury's Chalice Well

On a quiet, sunny afternoon in April, when a light mist was still in the air, some members of the Rosicrucian Order visited the garden of the Chalice Well and conducted a group meditation there. It was a sublime moment for them all. Legend says that the Grail in the form of the chalice brought there by Joseph of Arimathea, was lying in the depths of the Well. In moments like these, it really does not matter if the Grail is there, is not there, or could be there, or never was there. The mystique that has developed around the whole of Glastonbury through its atmosphere and its legends conditions one's mind to accepting the idea that the Grail is in the village, the site of the mystic Avalon, and what better place than the Chalice Well. The Well is located in a terraced garden-setting by the side of Chalice Hill. Its chalybeate and radioactive waters are believed to have healing properties, and the reddish water is said to be caused by the blood of Christ being mixed in it. This blend of Grail, the blood of Christ, and healing waters is a powerfully evocative compound symbol.

The visitor proceeds through the garden at three levels, along a narrow path, as if rising towards an inner sanctum of an open-air temple. On the right of the ascending path, a water channel from the Well takes the overflow of 25000 gallons per day out of the garden. The Well at the highest level is square and eight feet deep. Attached to the mouth of the Well is a cover which is usually kept open. The design on the cover is significant. The metal straps on its circular surface form a vesica piscis symbol, with a column or tree running through the middle of the two partly overlapping circles. We are told that this symbol was used for the geomantic siting of the sacred area around the cathedral. The supposed presence of the Grail in the Well, the tradition of its healing waters, and the more recent addition of the vesica piscis pattern on the well-cover, calls to mind the aspect of the Grail which characterises it as a wisdom cup, as the gnostic *sophia,* as the female counterpart of divinity.

The symbol on the cover can be read at various levels of understanding. The two circles represent the spiritual and mundane worlds which overlap to describe that moment when we feel the divine spark in us, when we feel that, though separate, we are still linked to the spiritual. It also stands for the constitution of mankind as being a composite of body (the material part) and soul (the immaterial part, spiritual part). The point of overlap can imply also that mystical moment when one receives a flash of illumination, and experiences the memory of a time when the two circles coincided; this could be the moment when one glimpses the Grail. The experience may be noetic and ecstatic, the moment when rebirth takes place.

Further interpretations of the symbol are intriguing. The shape of the overlap could be that of a fish, the sign of the early Christians who experienced Christ consciousness. Some see in it the shape of a temple which is the heart centre of mankind's contact with divinity. It is seen as a symbol of the Grail, and all that this implies. It also calls to mind the female generative organ and behind it the womb, with all the implications of creation and the maintenance of life. Many visitors have had "peak" experiences at the Well or during their stay at Glastonbury. If not, the symbol itself, visualised as one's personal Grail, could one day, and at an unexpected moment, wherever we are, have that beautiful experience which is best described by Jean Bolen as "vesica piscis experiences." They occur in our consciousness at those moments in and out of time "when the visible world and the invisible worlds intersect; when eternal values and the mundane world overlap; when the archetypal and the tangible world meet; when Heaven and Earth, the upper one and the lower one, come together in a liminal moment" (p. 119).

Some may think that *that* is the end of the quest for the Grail. In fact it is only the beginning! One becomes the Grail or is absorbed into it, when the overlap of the two circles ceases as they move into a common centre. It is this movement, and the truth it represents, that is contained in the mystery of the Grail Quest. Once the overlap occurs, as it did when Perceval beheld Arthur's knights in the forest and thought they were angels, today's Knight of the Grail must pick up their javelin, give their horse free rein, and ride through the valley!

Appendix 1
The Shaping of the Grail Myth

Some attempt will be made here, daunting though the task may be, to trace the evolving structure and content of the Knight in quest of the Grail, starting from conjecture on the original elements that form the background to the Myth, proceeding through the first written account which will be used as the skeleton of the romance, and adding the other parts of the "body' to complete its form as it has been handed down to us today. This conspectus will include mythological, psychological, mystical, religious and didactic aspects mentioned in this work, as well as the relevant contributions of primary authors and other secondary exposition or criticism. The content chosen is highly selective, and placed in note form. To do otherwise would require time-consuming analyses of the internal content of any work referenced, and that is not within the scope of this work.

The Grail Quest of Perceval is the most complete model of the Myth, and one which we can use for didactic purpose. That is, it is a unique presentation of the individual's search for the self, more so than Galahad's quest. Perceval starts from a low point and reaches lofty heights, Galahad is already half-way there, we see very little of his struggle. He is our earthly view of what mankind's spiritual state must be. We seem to learn from Galahad by being shown the pattern of what a Christian ascetic knight must become, but we learn much more from Perceval by tuning in to his experiences; for he is much like us, like humanity in general, who have to suffer and enjoy the life process in order to effect the process of spiritual alchemy that leads to the Grail. Both heroes have their individual appeal, but they are equal figures in the narrative, the aim of which is to exhort us to seek our true nature and purpose in relation to this planet and the cosmos. In order to centre our thought on this one character and the Grail object, it will be necessary to make only very brief and relevant references to other elements that colour the background of the Grail tradition, such as the experience of Gawain, Lancelot, Arthur, Guinevere and the whole Fellowship of the Round Table.

Suitable headings should prove valuable in fixing the sequence of events and shifts in thought. These will not necessarily follow a chronological order of appearance of the various Grail romances, since many of the dates are often approximations within a period of about fifty or so years. Rather, though the probable order of appearance will be taken into account, the emphasis would be on putting together the myth as a unified tale, and noting variations of interest from the four of five principal works that have been chosen for this reconstruction. Major primary works relating to the Grail are listed in Appendix 2.

A. The Precursors of the Grail and the Grail Quest.

1. Elements of ritual and myth in earlier mystery religions of the near east, and also the Megalithic rites associated with the Earth Goddess, and the Celtic mystery tradition which follow the latter, may be described as the precursors.

2. The cup or a stone as the sacred or magical object in the Grail romances has its counterparts in earlier religious cultures (Hindu, Buddhist, Hebrew, Egyptian, and shamanistic rituals).

3. Concepts of the Grail Temple probably developed from Megalithic structures, their orientation, siting and purpose, as early people attempted to contact and commune with supernatural forces or divinity; and also from places of worship in the Middle East (the Pyramids, Solomon's Temple, the Tabernacle, and even natural caves).

4. Closer to the Age of Chivalry, the "matter of Britain and Ireland", the oral tradition among the Druids, the legends of the quest and initiation, often having themes of vengeance, of magic cauldrons or horns of plenty, magical swords, spears, and other talismans, visits to the "otherworld", formed the resource background to the Grail myth that emerged in the 12th and 13th centuries.

5. *Peredur*, the Welsh version of *Perceval* was known about or before the time of Chrétien's written account, but it was not put into writing until its appearance in the *Mabinogion* in the 13th century. No Grail was mentioned in *Peredur*, but the ritual enacted included the display of a decapitated head on a platter.

6. The Chronicle of Helinandus (1204) indicates that the word "gradale", meaning a vessel, was known earlier than the time of the Grail poets.

B. The Shaping of the Grail Myth.

1. Chrétien de Troyes wrote his *Le Conte del Graal* (c. 1180—84), claiming his source to be a manuscript provided by his patron, Philip, Count of Flanders. The word Grail was used, but not clearly described, to indicate its form. Chrétien stated that it was of pure refined gold, it was set with precious stones, and that it outshone all the candles in the hall. The Grail was carried by a Grail Maiden, who was preceded by a youth carrying the lance which oozed blood from its tip, in a procession that entered and left the banquet hall. Just prior to this Perceval was also given a sword "that he was destined to have." The wounded Fisher King was present. Perceval failed to ask questions as to why the lance bled or who was served by the Grail. The poem was unfinished, and later completed, with variations, by continuators.

2. Robert de Boron's Joseph of Arimathea (c. 1190), and the later Vulgate Cycle of romances draw on apocryphal sources (the Gospel of Nicodemus and other Biblical references) to "establish" the Christian origin and nature of the Grail, but additional variations to the story were introduced by de Boron. The Grail was now the chalice of the last Supper, as well as the container of the blood of Christ, entrusted to Joseph of Arimathea, who brought it to England. A second square table was also made to celebrate the Sacraments in the manner of the Last Supper and using the original chalice. The Grail was thus "Holy", not simply magical, providing not only for the needs of the body but also for spiritual nourishment.

3. Part of the Vulgate contains a segment referred to as the *Petit Saint Graal*, or Lesser Holy Grail. In it the Fisher King's name was Bron, a relative of Joseph, who caught a fish that fed those at a mystic meal at Joseph's table. It is more than coincidence that the word Bron resembles Bran, a Celtic sea-god, made into a Welsh hero, and whose castle, Castell Dinas Bran, is claimed as the Welsh Grail Castle.

4. Robert de Boron stated that his source was a great book written by great clerics. In the three most important works on Perceval, those of Chrétien, de Boron, and Wolfram, all find authority in some yet undiscovered "book". The

original "book' may or may not have existed, or it may have been a story taking form in the Celtic or other oral tradition and was widely known.

5. Oriental Provenance of the Grail Story. Wolfram von Eschenbach, of the German cycle of Grail writers, claimed an oriental origin for the Grail story in his *Parzival* (c. 1210), and the Grail. is described as the stone that fell from Lucifer's crown. The stone's power was renewed every Good Friday, when a dove from heaven brought the host to it. It was however, a sad event for the Grail King, since it kept his wound fresh and left him alive. The poem broadly follows Chrétien's story, with minor variations, and adds to it the lives of his predecessors and son. Its importance, however, is its hermetic thought content.

6. The Perilous Seat. In the romances written or attributed to Robert de Boron, the Perilous Seat, a place to be left vacant as a reminder of the place Judas occupied during the Last Supper, was designated by the Holy Spirit as the seat at Joseph's table to discriminate between the unworthy and the pure of heart.

Later it became the seat at Arthur's Round Table for the knight destined to be the Grail hero. In Joseph's time, Moys sat on it and was swallowed up. Perceval attempted to sit on it, in the version called the Didot Perceval (Didot was the owner of the manuscript). The seat immediately split and a prophecy was made that Perceval and the Round Table Fellowship would suffer for it. The Celtic Perceval was in this sense "unseated" from his status as the Grail hero, a change which was confirmed in the *Queste del Saint Graal,* when Galahad, being imbued with the Holy Spirit, sat on it with no dire consequences, and was recognised as the rightful occupant.

7. Glastonbury as the Home of the Grail. Sometime after the Christianisation of the Grail by de Boron and the Vulgate scribes, Glastonbury, which had already been a "pagan" religious site and a centre of Celtic Christianity, and even later the place for an Abbey, soon became the home of the Grail. The romance called the *Perlesvaus,* or the High History of the Grail, was translated by Glastonbury monks. It states that the Grail was in Joseph's possession and mentions the spear of Longinus, the Roman centurion who pierced the body of Christ. The work is more allegorical than most and is highly symbolic. Kathleen Malwood's "Temple of the Stars" theory (1935) links the Glastonbury Zodiac

with the knight's encounters with fearsome creatures in places in the *Perlesvaus.* The Glastonbury Zodiac is Maltwood's discovery of coincidence of topographical and man-made features around Glastonbury with the heavenly Zodiac. If the writer of the romance had some astrological dimension to add to the knight's quest, this, together with his indirect references to the Grail knights being Templars, would find a close affinity with some of Wolfram's ideas. Both were alchemically inclined and sought correspondences between earth and heaven, seeing "the Grail message in the stars."

8. The *Grand Saint Graal (c.1212),* tells of Joseph's arrival in Glastonbury and of his burial there. The founding of an Order of Grail Knights is associated with the experiences of Joseph, his relatives and disciples before and after he set foot in Britain. So the concept of Grail Kingship or Grail Keepership was added to the legend. Mention is also made of the Grail being hidden in a castle. Glastonbury had no castle as such though it was a political and trading centre in Celtic and Roman times. But the castle as a safe place for the Grail is mentioned in more than one story.

9. Grail Knights — Wolfram von Eschenbach, in *Parzival* develops the Grail Kingship idea further. The qualification for the position included *lineage.* Perceval was himself an individual as well as a product of his ancestry, Titurel and Gahmuret. There were stories associated with them, as there was in the case of Perceval's son, Lohengrin. All carried a hereditary privilege and burden. They were all Keepers of the Grail.

In Wolfram, Grail superknights also guarded the Grail castle, and served on special missions. They were specially selected, were "bred to the pure life", and came from many lands. Wolfram's Grail Guardians were developed in the Age of Chivalry, and Joseph's original Grail Keepers were represented in the *Parzival* as Knights Templar. The Grail's home was not Glastonbury but a mountain fortress or temple in the Pyrenees.

Mystically, this group must be seen in the broader context of the human family and its evolvement, not as evidence of a racist theme or of a "chosen people" being promoted. Perceval, as well as Galahad, would be part of a spiritual bloodline by birth, just as we all are. What distinguishes them from us is the assumption that there are in the broad mass of humanity some who have realised this divine connection sooner and have chosen to make it change the pattern of their lives. To put it another way, they are in the eternal presence of the Grail. Either of the two heroes present images of the "new man", come to restore man to his original state. The attempt to add more into this than the allegorical, as is well known, has proved disastrous in our time.

Wolfram introduced hermetic and alchemical themes into his work, e.g., the contrasts of light and darkness, good and evil, the potentiality of either value being present in any human act, the choice of light in moments of moral uncertainty, and the evolvement of humans through personal effort, doubt and suffering.

Richard Wagner takes up the mystical theme in his operas. He makes the Grail King, Amfortas, the son of Titurel, who is the perfect servant of the Grail in heaven. Titurel is the higher self, and Amfortas, the fallen man. Titurel remains in the background in the opera, *Parsifal*, as a voice. Parsifal is the renewing force which grows in proportion to the dying earthly aspects in Titurel (the self in Amfortas), which ends in Parsifal achieving Titurel's original state (the self, freed of its burden).

C. Stage 1 of the Perceval Story

1. Boyhood and Early Youth.

a) Perceval is brought up by his mother who has retreated to the forest to escape from a world of human conflict which has caused the death of her kinsmen. The child is brought up in a different environment to that of other children of royalty or nobility.

Forest and Mother are merged symbols. Represented here are aspects of the Mother Goddess, the creative, caring and nourishing principles in nature. Both represent the archetype of the "mother", one on a macrocosmic and the other on a microcosmic scale. Perceval's mother Herzeleide (Heart's Sorrow) shows the positive aspects of the archetype, as described above. In the negative aspect, she is unresponsive to the masculine need for fulfillment of that part of his nature, and is overly protective. In her sorrow, she is a poor mediator for the self.

c) The forest is also identified with the unconscious, as indeed is the feminine component of our own psyche, which again is equated with the soul in man. Both forest and the feminine are mysterious, the enigmatic content of this segment of the psyche has to be sounded, understood, and given due consideration in the operations of the conscious mind.

d) Perceval is in a state of innocence, attuned to nature and the feminine. But in boyhood and early youth he is egocentric, socially inept, yet responsive to the suffering of lower animals, and to his inner impulses. When he is seen to be a "Fool", he performs inconsiderate acts, but is not prompted by malice.

2. Separation from Mother

a) His first view of Arthur's knights in the forest is dramatic, he mistakes them for angels. This is his first intuitive contact with the Grail, though he is unaware of it. His aspiration is still limited, he wants to become one of Arthur's knights. Yet the company is a select one, it is these knights who would later seek the Grail.

b) In Wagner's opera *Parsifal* this encounter is regarded as the first awakening of his union with divinity, the first memory of being separate from something he was. It may also be described as his first initiatory threshold to be crossed, that of being "called to the Grail" and of being ready. The second initiatory stage include his later experiences up to the meeting with the hermit, and the third, the attainment of Grail Kingship.

3. Experiences as the "Fool": Episode of the Lady in the Tent.

a) In Chrétien's *Le Conte du Graal* and in most versions of the tale, Perceval shows rough and irresponsible behaviour, what we may describe today in legal terms as assault and robbery, with insult added, on the gentle innocence of a sleeping lady. In the Welsh *Peredur,* he is actually received graciously by the Lady receiving both a kiss and her ring and is duly impressed by kindness. She is in fact bestowing sovereignty, or a recognition of it, in respect to his later status.

b) The Pavilion and the Lady in the Tent (named "Jeshute" in Wolfram) is symbolically interpreted by some as a re-enactment of a Biblical event of the violation of Solomon's Temple in AD 70. One has to view the Perceval quest as representative of mankind in general. The sacred place (the Pavilion as the Temple) was desecrated by human ignorance and self-will; so the journey back to wholeness, the restitution of injuries imposed, and the return to divinity, is made much harder.

4. Experiences of the "Fool": The Contest with the Red Knight.

a) The Red Knight was Perceval's "shadow", which is repressed rather than accommodated. The Red Knight's behaviour was not unlike Perceval's at this stage.

b) The skilful use of the javelin shows singularity of purpose. But he acted in haste, disregarding the rules of chivalry (as he did not know these), and later found out that the Red Knight was a relative (in Wolfram, he is Perceval's uncle Ither).

c) Perceval's *persona,* or social mask is developed; the shadow is thrust back. This is symbolized by Perceval putting on the armour of the Red Knight over his old clothes. He has not become a knight, only the pretence of one.

d) Red Armour and regalia are not always to be regarded as a negative symbol. Galahad, who appears in the *Queste del Saint Graal* wore red armour as an outward sign of the blood of the Saviour, the blood of love and life.

5. The Knights' Code: Induction into Chivalry.

a) Gournemanz, an experienced knight, becomes Perceval's mentor and instructs him in the knightly virtues. He is the social discipline component of the "wise man" archetype. The rules of the group are given pre-eminence over impulsive, instinctual drives.

b) This is Perceval's first initiation into fellowship; he is shown tribal skills of survival within the group and his mastery of these guarantees acceptance by the group.

c) The method includes training by verbal instruction and demonstration of skills, help in interpretation of past experiences and opportunities given for introspection, and constant encouragement. Initiation takes place within the core of his nature: attitudes of consideration and compassion develop, together with control over impulses and instinctual drives.

d) The next level to be reached — the development of higher values than chivalry — is self-realisation. One has to move above social adjustment and total submission to group conformity. At a higher level one tries to live authentically; on the one hand, by not being a slave to one's desires, and on the other, by being prepared to step beyond the rules or conventions of the group. There remains the question about the extent to which instincts have to be controlled and the extent to which one diverges from the group. One can rationalise one's behaviour to include unrestricted freedom in the former case, or in the latter, extreme divergence to the point of social isolation. The debate will continue, seeing that rationality and moral exhortation have so far failed to provide the total answer. To the mystic, who has reached this higher level of consciousness, the solutions are to be found in experience, reflection, and response to the intuitions from the individual's inner world.

6. Experiencing Love

a) After he has done her a service, Blanchefleur (Chrétien's 'White Flower'), or Condwiramur (Wolfram's 'Stream of Love'), is courted by Perceval, and they marry. He passes through the phase of seeing her as his projected ideal and as a real person. Their love is at two levels, spiritual and earthly, it takes them three days to become intimate. In Perceval's psyche at this moment his animus and anima coexist in perfect harmony. But unlike other tales, the end point is not "happiness ever after". There is the matter of the Grail.

b) Perceval makes two reluctant departures from those very close to him — from his friend Gournemanz, and from his wife, Blanchefleur. The highest virtue may include separation from, or temporary sacrifice of, the personal happiness and connubial love, in order to correct past mistakes, to submit to one's conscience. The stated reason for his departure was to return to his mother, unaware that she has already died. The "Grail of the Heart" is operating very strongly at this level, for compassion and love at its finest must be universal, not limited.

c) In Wagner's *Parsifal* the hero's experiences (e.g. deep sorrow for having killed the swan, his anguish at hearing the King's cries, and his rejection by Gournemanz), open the way for the development of a higher love, and stand him in good stead in the next Act, when he has to overcome the magic of Klingsor and the seductions of a Kundry in disguise, and capture the sacred lance from Klingsor.

7. The River, or Expanse of Water

The River is a strong symbol; it is a frontier between the physical world and the spiritual or invisible worlds, and is not crossed easily. In a Breton legend of Lancelot, he is abducted in infancy by the Lady of the Lake, taken under the water of the Lake, beyond reach of his parents, and there spends his boyhood and youth before emerging into the physical world. The lake may be seen here as the depths of the *mind.* When Perceval first met the Grail King the latter appeared as a Fisherman, fishing in its waters to find a healing agent_for his wound.

Fish in the water are a source of food and symbolically represent the source of wisdom in the unconscious. As food nourishes a body in need of sustenance, so does wisdom heal or refine the ignorant ego.

The nature of this frontier is also described in a related symbol, the *vesica piscis.* It is the meeting point and point of overlap of two circles, of two worlds, the visible and the invisible. The meeting point symbolises our momentary contact with, or our partial immersion in, a new level of consciousness, described as a "peak" experience by Maslow, and liminal experience by Bolen. The experience gives greater depth to our understanding of reality and transforms our attitudes towards the human and natural world.

The Wounded Fisherman fishing in the waters is explained in religious terms as the attempt of man to return from his present fallen state to his original state in paradise.

Perceval was "deflected" from his journey home to his mother, because of the hidden call of the Grail. There was work to be done, other experiences and trials to encounter. He was "invited" to, but really was expected at, the castle of the Grail; he, that is his conscious, rational mind, did not intend to go there, but on reaching the frontier between his conscious and unconscious he found himself responsive to certain archetypal energies of the unconscious.

D. Stage II: The Second Level of Initiation.

This is the hero's first contact with the invisible, Celtic "Otherworld." The first mystical contact with a different reality is a profound shift in consciousness. The experience is sudden, catching the initiate unawares. But preparation (Perceval's experiences and change of heart) was a necessary part of the process. In theological terms, it is the Christian grace of God granted for strict obedience to His will, and sometimes even without this precondition, as it may appear to us. To the Celtic mind, such grace comes after personal striving, commitment, holding the right motives and facing certain tests —wherever the grace comes from, it is earned and then granted.

1. The Grail Castle and Kingdom.

a) This is the Celtic "Otherworld", a world of enchantment, another world into which mortals may move in and out, and encounter its inhabitants. It is another dimension of human experience.

b) The Otherworld makes sense to us, if we regard it as the mysterious unconscious of our psyche. If we imagine it as unexplored territory, travel to and from it expands or raises our level of consciousness.

c) The Grail Castle is described in Wolfram's *Der Junge Titurel (c. 1215),* as one that was topped with a rose carbuncle; in the *Sone of Nansai (c. 1250* a poet of Brabant) as a castle on an island off the Norwegian coast, in Albrecht von

Scharfenberg's *Die Jungere Titurel (c. 1270)* as a Temple Palace in Persia; and in the *Queste del Saint Graal* the location is the (to us unlocatable) Castle of *Corbenic.* This word has been etymologically interpreted as "blessed horn" or "blessed raven", where there is a suggestion of link with Bran, the Welsh Grail King and also as "blessed body" where the Christian influence relates it to the sacred body of Christ.

d) One may also mystically conceive the visit to the Grail castle as a visit to the centre of one's being, the meeting point of heaven and earth in the human consciousness. The most entrancing symbolic expression of this idea is that of a high mountain, tipped with snow and ringed with clouds, its peak surmounted by the Grail castle, reaching up to heaven. Montségur in the French Pyrenees would fit this image in winter, and is quite impressive at other times. Hence the interest of "Nordic" or "Polar" scholars and archaeologists in the area of Ariège in the first half of this century.

e) Perceval's entry into the Grail castle. — Whereas the Grail allegorically speaking, visited Perceval in the form of knightly "angels" in his youth and started him off on his quest, admission into the Grail castle found him in its presence and nourished by it. This is his first touch of illumination, and he was dumbfounded. This is generally explained as unreadiness, or unworthiness, or ignorance, or misunderstanding of the rules of knightly courtesy. It may be better understood in terms of the mystical experience which, when it occurs for the first time, imposes an awesome silence on the one going through the experience. This was also a part of the initiatory process in the Mysteries; the candidate was exposed to certain events and movements in the ritual, and was shown or given certain sacred objects, all conveying some deep meaning. The candidate for initiation was expected to respond in some way by answering or asking questions. The hierophants of the Mysteries decided when a candidate was ready. This is why Perceval did not find the Grail castle, nor he was looking for it particularly; he was on his way to his mother. It was the Fisherman who thought that Perceval was the knight who was destined to use the power of the Grail to lift the spell on the King and the Land. He was, but that wasn't the moment.

f) The Grail Queen. — Sovereignty is bestowed on Perceval in the other "Otherworld". Unaware of it, he is declared to be the future Grail King. The Queen puts her cloak around his shoulders, raising him from his apparent humble origins. The feminine principle assumes its mediating role for the self. In the legends where Arthur is given more focus, Guinevere plays the role of Sovereignty, conferring legitimacy to Arthur as King. As a Celtic queen she also has the right to have more than one lover. By Christian standards, however, she was judged to be an adulteress, and Lancelot a dishonoured knight. For this, both spent the rest of their lives in penitence.

g) The Grail King.

i) The Wounded King/Wasteland nexus is of ancient origin; the image presents the belief that the health and vitality of the king is directly related to the fertility of the land and the welfare of his subjects. Replacement of the king was necessary when he, or the land failed to live up to expectations, and this was usually cyclic, often tied to seasonal change or to a certain number of years. In some cases a king was a god on earth or his representative, and this idea seems to have been carried forward into the present when students of the Grail Myth come to regard the Fisher King being symbolically God himself, and Perceval the figure of Christ. The Grail romances do not express or imply this, however, for in all cases the King is either extremely old and impotent, or Wounded (with an implication of sexual impotence due to being wounded in the thighs or genitals).

ii) The King is better represented in religious terms as the once perfect, original man, of Adam before the Fall, who is now the wounded, imperfect, suffering, degenerate or fallen man.

iii) In de Boron's *Joseph of Arimathea (c.1200),* and in Henrich von dem Türlin's *Diu Krône* (c.1230), he is simply an old man needing renewal. In the latter romance, Gawain and not Perceval is the hero.

iv) Chrétien's *Le Conte* (c. 1180) has two kings, one old and weak and the other perfect, showing two aspects of the one being, the ideal man and the degenerate man. It is Perceval's destiny or task to reach the state of ideal man by healing the imperfect one.

v) Greed and lust provide the reason for the Grail King's wound and the land being waste, as it is told in the *Elucidation (c. 1315).* The wells as the source of water for a fertile and bountiful land ran dry when the Grail Amangons and his followers ravished the Maidens of the Wells who cared for the wells and refreshed travellers who passed by. The moral lapse in the King is seen also as a split with nature.

vi) Wolfram, in his *Parzival* calls the Grail King Amfortas (the infirm), who succumbed to the temptations of Klingsor, the Magician (material pleasures). He allowed the lance to become separated from the chalice and was wounded by Klingsor using the same lance. It was rightly a healing lance, but was used punitively when it was lost to Klingsor. An attempt to use it destructively against Perceval failed, for he succeeded in rising above his desire nature. Perceval caught the lance in flight, and being in the right hands, it was used soon after to heal the Wounded King.

vii) The *Queste del Saint Graal (c. 1215—30)* has Pelles and his father bearing the title of Grail King. The Wound in his thigh was caused by the breaking of taboos relating to Solomon's ship and the Sword of David. This was a further Cistercian attempt to bring Grail mythology into line with Biblical imagery. The King is healed by Galahad, but this does not end the Galahad quest, as it did with the earlier romances. In the *Queste,* Galahad was marked to be the Grail hero from the very start, when he sat on the Perilous Seat. In the final moments of his quest, as he headed for Sarras (Jerusalem), he was on Solomon's ship and had the Grail in his keeping. At Sarras, the Grail is taken to heaven, and he himself passes to a higher stage of initiation, where he is united with God.

viii) In the *Perlesvaus* (c. *1190—1212)* the anonymous writer hints at the condition of the Fisher King as being a weakness of *will.* The Grail King dies before Perceval completes the Quest, thus removing the inconsistency of the Old King being healed, in which case Perceval would have no need to displace, but to replace, him.

ix) In some commentaries on Arthur and the Round Table Fellowship, Arthur's story is patterned on the Grail King/Wasteland myth, again to draw attention to the verities about human nature. Arthur brought peace and happiness to Britain by keeping the barbarians without, and justice within, his kingdom. But he could no longer keep his fellowship of knights together through human frailty in himself and in those who were close to him. Ultimately, he failed to undertake leadership in the Grail Quest. With the return of civil disorder and disunity, the misery of the Wasteland returned and people awaited a renewed or re-healed "once and future king."

2. The Grail Procession in the Banquet Hall

The Grail Procession is the central event used in the argument that Grail literature was a record of the ritual of an extant mystery cult "surviving under conditions of strict secrecy."

a) A Maiden, not a priest, was the Grail Bearer. A youth bore the spear which dripped blood, suggesting the ritual was of a fertility cult. The Christian mystery is suggested as an upgrade of this cult, taking the magical aspect of the vegetation mysteries to a higher spiritual level. The cup and contents of Christ's redeeming blood point to the majestic and sacrificial nature of the creative and redemptive process. One can also notice a Catharistic element here. Cathar leadership saw no distinction between men and women. The ritual of the Grail Procession was recording this acknowledgment of the importance of the feminine principle in human development, which was compensating for the patriarchal emphasis given in orthodox Christianity. A hint of a secret tradition appearing in Grail literature is also suggested in the *Perlesvaus*. In it, the Grail is described in five manifesting images, which could be interpreted as showing aspects of Christ from birth to crucifixion, or other stages of initiation in another cult, without any reference to the Christian mystery.

b) The movements and sequences arranged, and the objects displayed, are meant to be revelations to the hero initiate, who is expected to ask a specific question or questions, which would indicate the level of his advancement in the mystery and also his acceptance into a status within the cult.

c) The strongest case for the Grail romances being a record of a mystery ritual going back to oriental mystery cults was made by Jessie Weston. Her thesis has been disputed, however, on the grounds of it being inadequate to explain the whole phenomenon of the appearance of Grail literature in the twelfth and thirteenth centuries. This is unfortunate, since it argues cogently and with sufficient historical evidence to establish at least a probable connection between the literature and the secret cultic groups, who, by their need to maintain secrecy make research more difficult. And she offered her insights without claims to receive her knowledge from "higher", unverifiable sources.

3. The Grail Secret.

a) Whether a platter, cup, stone or book or symbolic representation of an idea or truth, it still is, as it then was, a mystery, to be apprehended in a special way. The *Elucidation (c. 1315),* cautions against revealing the secret; it carries a threat of dire consequences. When spoken about by those who know the secret it had to be done with scrupulous accuracy and only uttered by a holy person. Those who listened would tremble at the knowledge of it. Again, we have here a reminder of similar injunctions used by mystery schools or secret brotherhoods. Secrecy was imposed upon initiates to ensure that their sacred knowledge would not be profaned.

b) Conjectures on the secrets of the Grail are listed below:

i) The Grail as a symbol tells of the meaning and process of life and creation. Woman, as the human form of the Goddess is given a preeminent role here. The combination of Grail Maiden bearing a cup symbolises, from the very beginnings, the transformative character of the Grail going_hand in hand with the creative forces of nature and in physical and sublimated man. Women know the secret, they live it, they are the teachers of the mystery and guides to men who seek to know the secret.

ii) The use of a vessel and its contents concretised this concept in mythology. Celtic magical cauldrons were food providers, they could heal or poison, they could regenerate life. The vessel was an inexhaustible source that gave life and sustained it by its magical contents. Spiritual nourishment and inner transformation through the blood of Christ became the emphasis in the period of the Grail romances. The Grail here is the understanding of the Christian mystery, and perhaps, of other ancient mysteries.

iii) The secret could be seen in Wolfram's *Parzival* as a stone of wisdom, revelation and transformation.

Though this idea is oriental and hermetic, Christian symbolism is also added: a dove brought the host down from heaven and replenished the powers of the stone, again revealing Wolfram's desire to reconcile religious differences. This annual act of the host empowering the stone could be interpreted as the constant effort of divinity to maintain its presence in Creation, as a companion to man in his wounded state. The Wounded King was being kept alive by this act against his will, so long was his period of suffering, The old self had to die, nevertheless, so that the new self, in the form of Perceval, might rise from the alchemical "blackness", in its purified form. The secret of the Grail is its power to make the phoenix rise from its ashes after being consumed by intense heat. It may be the sacrificial blood of the saviour, represented in the symbol of the pelican who tears open its breast to feed its young; life is born out of sacrifice and maintained by sacrifice. It is the philosopher's stone, which Wolfram was hinting at, which was the agent of transmutation of imperfect metals into gold, and which conveyed the message of human transformation or redemption.

iv)If Perceval's experience, up to the visit to the Grail castle, represented the vicissitudes and successes in life as his exposure to the "lesser mysteries", then the witnessing of the Grail cup in the Grail Procession, calls attention to the Grail as an alchemical retort, the means of spiritual regeneration, or Perceval's first exposure to the "higher mysteries." The secret of the Grail is also the secret of the Grail Quest: "lesser" and "higher" taken together chart the progress of the individual soul through experience gained by living the purposeful life.

4. The Lance and the Lance Bearer

a) In the Celtic context, the lance is the fiery and destructive spear of Lugh which always finds its target, or the spear of victory. It is compared with lightning, recalling the death-dealing power of the thunderbolt, or in mystical terms, as flashes of cosmic insight. In the *Queste de Saint Graal* it caused the Dolorous Stroke that put the land of Logres, (England) under an evil spell, so that it became a waste land. Another story tells of its use as a destroyer, it was the cause of Mordred's death. Under Christian influence, it became the healing weapon (in the Vulgate version), dipped in the healing blood of the Saviour. A rare Celtic parallel occurs where the drops of magic fluid from Keridwen's cauldron (which started a train of events resulting in the rebirth of Gwion as Taliesin), and the drops of blood that fell from the tip of the lance held by the bearer in the Grail.

Procession. The drops of magic fluid from the cauldron and the blood from the body of Christ both told the same story of healing and transformation.

b) Wolfram also interposes the incident of the Wounded Swan (although an arrow, which is similar to a lance, was used) and the drops of blood on the white surface of the snow. Parzival goes into a trance on seeing this, deep in meditation, in which he sees, in the face and tears of Condwiramur, a spiritual love.

c) Wagner, in taking up the theme of the lance, makes Parsifal, on the threshold of his elevation in the Kingdom of the Grail, kneel before the spear he has thrust into the ground and starts to pray or meditate. This act symbolically represents the contact made between Parsifal and the earth and cosmos, the centre within, the *axis mundi*, in the temple of his heart, with consequent changes in his nature, after which he sees the world differently and becomes the Healer. Wilmshurst, in his monograph on *Parsifal* identifies the lance with the will of God, or the life force which, along with the Grail, sustained the Grail King and Kingdom. The return of the lance by Parsifal to its place by the chalice is the important theme in this opera. The separation of divine will from the chalice of love by the misapplied will of man, keeps man distant from the Creator.

5. The Sword

a) 'The sword is given to the hero in the Grail castle in some versions; in others, he is expected to bring two parts of the weapon together as a test of his right to keep it and use its power for good.

b) The act of receiving or gaining the sword symbolises that the initiate on the mystic quest acquires the ability to discriminate in judgement, to mix or not mix emotions in making difficult decisions. But it is only one power to be used in the rehabilitation of the disturbed or wounded psyche.

c) In the *Queste,* Galahad was the only knight who could draw the sword from the stone, signifying the inner purity that merited such privilege; it was much like Arthur's sword that established his right to be King of England, and also the sword that he received from the Lady of the Lake which gave power to that right and established his sovereignty.

6. The Question.

a) It is characteristic of the mysteries that one is expected to answer or ask questions, questions that would lead one to an understanding of the mystery. In Perceval's case the question had to be asked at the right moment (that is, when he saw the Sick King on the couch, or when he saw the bleeding lance, or set eyes on the wondrous object called the Grail), and with the right motives. In this way the initiate is tested. It has to be a spontaneous act, not socially learned, and coming from the promptings of the inner self.

b) Self-examination by introspection and reflection is a necessary part of raising the level of one's consciousness.

c) In legend the effect of asking the question is also macrocosmic. The question asked by a single individual would have healed the King and restored the barren land. It raises another question of one's individual responsibility in influencing the course of events, or the state of the planet, or the general state of humanity.

d) The critical moment when big decisions have to be made is not always the moment chosen by ourselves or others. The attempt to accelerate the process of change in the Kingdom of the Otherworld or in Perceval's consciousness was a bit premature. Or perhaps it was a test, since it is not always possible to know in advance one's level of understanding. Failure to ask the first question "What ails thee, uncle?" or "Why does the lance bleed?" would indicate that he was not compassionate enough. And failure to ask the question "Whom does the Grail serve?" revealed that he was psychically unable, in that state of innocence, to face the questions concerning his own destiny.

7. The Loathsome Creature or Kundry (in Wolfram).

a) She is a Grail Messenger, another form of the Goddess, She is the conveyor of *truth* which breaks hypocrisy and the ethics of social expediency. She persuades Parsifal to abandon his courtly life and resume the personal quest, and she does this by public chastisement. Truth may look ugly and cause shame, but its inherent beauty is veiled.

b) This faerie figure is to be found in other legends. For instance, Gawain has a similar experience which illustrates his virtue of loyalty and love for Arthur. He kisses an ugly creature in order to save Arthur from the embarrassment of keeping a promise. Here was true sacrifice. The beauty of his act was correspondingly rewarded when the "beast" was transformed by a kiss into a beautiful woman.

c) In Wolfram's poem, Kundry is a seducer acting for Klingsor, and she is presented in the negative and positive aspects of the feminine. She attempts to turn man from his true nature, testing him, to see if he can surmount his physical desires. Wagner shows Kundry and Gournemanz also raised to a higher level of consciousness as a result of Perceval's triumph over Klingsor and the return of the lance to the Grail Castle, giving strength to the idea that every individual's victory over his lower nature has its effect on humanity as a whole.

In Wolfram and Wagner the Zoroastrian doctrine of the constant and bitter conflict between the forces of Light and the Forces of Darkness, of Good and Evil, is presented in sharper contrast here than in the other Grail romances. The exhortation that every man has to play his part in this universal struggle on the side of the good is given great focus and intensity. Kundry has been enticed into the service of Klingsor and his dark forces working against the Grail Kingdom, the "forces" implied being the pleasures of the flesh, the enchantment that goes with these, self-pride, and malice. The dice seem loaded against the Grail Kingdom, until Perceval tipped the balance, by resisting these seductions, and capturing the sacred lance which Klingsor hurled at him. This marked the end of Klingsor as an evil force, the salvation of Kundry, the healing of the King's wound with the lance and the acceptance of Perceval as the new Grail King.

8. Gawain and the "Continuations".

a) Chrétien's *Le Conte du Graal* remains unfinished after Perceval's attendance at Arthur's court and his meeting with the Loathsome Creature. The remainder of the poem deals with Gawain's adventures. The introduction of Gawain as a second hero has been explained in various ways, to wit, that he is Perceval's double who proceeds according to rules of knighthood, in contrast to

Perceval who strives to reach a higher level of consciousness; or that Gawain was originally the Grail hero in the yet unwritten legend, more archaic than Perceval, and that Perceval replaced him; or that it may have been slotted into the main tale simply for additional interest by Chrétien or some other poet, since their appearances in the story are not intertwined and it seems as if two stories were brought under the one title.

b) Four Continuators have attempted to complete the story left unfinished by Chrétien, one dealing with the adventures of Gawain, and the others with Perceval's final adventures and his attainment to Grail Kingship. These are referred to as the Four Continuations, or by the names of their authors or pronable authors: the Pseudo-Wauchier, that of Wauchier de Denan (c. 1200), the Manessier and Gerbert de Montreul versions (c. 1200—30).

9. The "Dark Night of the Soul"

a) After his failure at the Grail castle and his return to the normal world, Perceval enters a period of despair and loss of faith, contrasting with the momentary bliss of his experiences in the "otherworld". He has plunged into the "Dark Night", when he loses a sense of purpose, and wanders through the wilderness for another five years, simply acting as a knight and sometimes following his intuitions.

b) In alchemy this is described as the *nigredo* phase, a state of "blackness", in order that the hermetically sealed vessel, time and heat, may engender the "stone" that would separate the pure from the impure stuff and produce the philosopher's gold. Perceval was going through this process of internal pain for his final illumination.

c) The "Dark Night" is also suggested in Wolfram and Wagner to explain the condition of the Grail King and his unhappy kingdom. It has strong Biblical undertones: it points to the separation of man from his true (that is, divine) nature and how the return may be effected. The "How?" is what the Perceval story is about.

E. Stage III: The Transition to Transcendence.

1. Meeting with the Hermit Trevrizent.

a) When sufficient time had elapsed to allow for the necessary incubation to take place, the final reconstitution of disordered elements of Perceval's experiences takes place with the help of the hermit Trevrizent. It is a period of inner healing brought about by compassion and understanding from another source, a male figure, the "wise old man" with a spiritual dimension.

b) Trevrizent is a hermit, having retired from his knightly service and court life to pursue the life of the spirit. He is the hierophant of the mysteries, who has been through the full circle of experience and has "been beyond." He can therefore conduct Perceval's final initiation for admission to the Grail Kingdom. He is not a priest, but performs priestly functions in respect to Perceval's conversion. The influence of Grail Christianity is strong here, as it is in the legends of this period when the mystic living in isolation is contrasted with the communal life of monks, and when hermitages become places of rest, refuge, and advice to travellers in their moments of passage through life.

c) For Perceval, his stay with the hermit marks a phase of humility, of contrition, of promise, and transition through the threshold to a higher level of consciousness.

2. The Second Visit to the Grail Castle.

a) This is the phase of new-found confidence, of the moment when the hermetic seal has been removed, of enlightenment, of transcendence, of the completion of the journey to a mysterious oneness with divinity.

b) Perceval has passed all tests, he becomes the healer, a saviour, because of his acquired powers flowing from the Grail. He represents mankind returned to a former state of bliss.

c) The Wasteland is made fertile and bountiful and its people once more enter a golden age, because the rift between human nature and nature has been repaired.

d) If Perceval and the Wounded King are seen as two aspects of the one being, then the former was the exteriorised model for the interior suffering latter, while the latter typified the thrust of life attempting renewal.

e) Psychologically, Perceval's final initiation represents the human psyche in a state of harmony, of wholeness, of integration, of self-realisation. It applies in a collective sense as well: the human species in cooperation will have to shape its destiny by redefining its ideals and values, if only for our survival as a species on this planet.

f) In the *Queste del Saint Graal* we have the fully Christianised version of the Grail Quest. Galahad's final elevation does not occur in the Grail Castle of Celtic faerie, but at Sarras (thought to be Jerusalem, as the Holy City and therefore a Grail Kingdom on Earth). And there, since he had contemplated "the mysteries of the Grail" his soul was released from the body and borne by angels to Heaven. The Grail and Lance were also lifted up to Heaven "for ever". This firm statement has not however, prevented the many seekers from setting out on the quest for the actual or imaginary object called the Grail right up to our day!

Galahad returned to the divine source. And whereas Perceval had to go through various trials and levels of advancement to reach his "otherworld", Galahad in the *Queste* appeared saintly from the moment he entered the hall of the Round Table; already it would seem at a high level of consciousness. In the Cistercian ethos he was made to be an ascetic, Christlike person, to supplant Perceval as the most successful Grail knight. Described sometimes as a cardboard figure, many would find it easier to empathise with Perceval as a more realistic model of ebb and flow of human energy in the quest for the ideal. The difference between the two knights is noted when Galahad, not Perceval, was able to sit on the Perilous Seat without any mishap and was recognised as the purest knight. It is confirmed when, at the final stages of the story, the Grail King episode appears only as minor compared with the final journey in Solomon's ship, with Galahad being the assigned Keeper of the Grail who is to take it to Sarras, ending with his ascent to Heaven. Perceval and Bors simply accompany him.

g) The three acts of Wagner's music-drama *Parsifal* covers the following events, sequences, and character modifications to suit his medium of presentation, but they do not alter the essence of the myth and even gives its strong mystical dimension.

Act I. Forest scene and Grail castle, Gournemanz described the Grail King's suffering, Perceval shoots down a swan and is chastised for it, Kundry relates Perceval's family history, the uncovering of the chalice, and Gournemanz rejection of Perceval for his failure to act as he was expected. This is described as Parsifal's first awakening of his consciousness to the memory of his divine source.

Act II:. Klingsor's tower, the garden, Klingsor himself and Kundry all feature in the attempted seduction of Perceval. Perceval successfully resists all temptations thrust at him; he captures the sacred spear thrown at him by Klingsor in anger instead of being pierced by it, and the whole world of Klingsor collapses. The scene is meant to demonstrate the various processes of transcendental alchemy.

Act III. Gournemanz is here seen as playing the role of the hermit, his attitude has changed. Kundry, too, is now penitent. Both are transformed when Perceval returns to heal the ailing king and redeem the Brotherhood of the Holy Grail. He has attained mastership in the mystic quest and can use the power of the Grail to aid the rest of humanity.

h) Wagner's great purpose was mystical, He implied that behind all the literary romances developing various aspects of the Grail theme, the most important message was that there existed in a part of humanity a hierarchy of Grail Guardians — those of highly developed spiritual consciousness — dedicated to transform humanity. He implied also that there was an esoteric way to enter into this process of transformation, and that it required discipline among those who followed the path of the dedicated that leads to the Grail, to a reintegration with divinity. By combining all the components of theatre, he revived the troubadour tradition of entertainment and instruction in our time. Thus he justified his inclusion into that company, that hierarchy of souls who come down from the heights of Montsalvat to help those who are camped below.

To conclude we may say that the Grail myth, which is a composite of the

Hero's Quest, a Wounded Grail King, and a magical or sacred object, arose in man's consciousness as an attempt to understand and manage, or come to terms with, the forces within his own psyche and those present in the environment. The truth being presented is that, when there is disharmony between human nature and nature, where nature is being treated as a "thing" and not personalised and treated accordingly, there is need to restore the balance, both for the sake of nature and for mankind. The reverse also applies. We tend to treat people or other living creatures as things to be exploited, instead of regarding them as an extension of ourselves, and as participants in the variety and beauty of a mysterious universe.

Myth may be unhistorical, but the recurrent nature of specific myths in different cultures, points to a truth different from that provided from the facts of history, often even stronger in effect, since it is apprehended at deeper levels of our understanding. An important message that this myth shares with others is its presentation of the theme of decline, age, and death, the need for renewal of the old and inefficient, of the weakened spirit by the '*new man'*, a new spirit, and the inevitability of change in the life process. Individually, the wound and the unhappy position of the king and his subject may be explained as the chronic disharmony and pain felt in the psyche through its inability to reconcile the splits within its total dynamic. At the collective level, the myth bears a message of caution and hope. We must rise above our limitations and take more care of ourselves as a species along with other forms of life, and generally protect this planet from misuse or the depletion of its resources.

In religious terms, the Quest and the Wounded King nexus is a dramatic presentation in poetry, prose, or music of the theme of the redemption of man from a fallen state, by allowing divine will to guide one's actions (represented by the lance) and experiencing divine love (symbolized by the Grail). On the mystical side, the whole quest for the Grail can be regarded as an allegory on the whole range of consciousness experienced by the individual from the lowest to the highest level. The highest level, the level of the Grail, is of course that state of consciousness experienced as One, the experience of total reality, beyond this world of illusion. One tastes the contents of the Grail when there is harmony within one's self and harmony in its relationship with nature and the cosmos, and one steps through the threshold of transpersonal and transcendent experience.

Appendix 2
Primary Works on the Grail Myth

Probable or Actual Dates Of Appearance	Title and Comments	Author
1180 or 1184	Le Conte du Graal (Essentially Celtic)	Chrétien de Troyes
c.1200+	Le Roman de L'Histoire dou Graal or Joseph of Arimathea (Christian, Cistercian influence)	Robert de Boron
	The First Continuation of "le Conte" (Gawain's adventures)	The Pseudo Wauchier
	The Second Continuation (more of Perceval)	Wauchier de Denan
	The Third Continuation (conclusion of Grail castle visit)	Manessier
	The Fourth Continuation (alternative to Manessier)	Gerbert de Montreuil
c.1191-1212	Perlesvaus or The High History of the Grail (allegorical, symbolic, astrological)	Anonymous
1210	Parzival (Christian references but hermetic, oriental,universal)	Wolfram von Eschenbach
c.1212	Le Grand Saint Graal (other titles: The Book of the Holy Grail, Le Saint Graal, The First Branch of Romances of The Round Table)	Probably a cleric from Cluny
1215	Der Junge Titurel	Wolfram von Eschenbach

Probable or Actual Dates Of Appearance	Title and Comments	Author
1215-1230	The Vulgate Cycle (includes: L'Histoire del Saint Graal Lancelot (Galahad introduced) La Queste del saint Graal (Galahad's story)	Walter Map (disputed) or anon Cistercian cleric
c.1225	Vulgate Merlin, Huth Merlin, Prophecies of Merlin	Anonymous
1230	Diu Krône	Heinrich von dem Türlin
c.1250	Sone of Nansai (sometimes spelt Nausai)	A poet from Brabant
c.1270	Der Jungere Titurel	Albrecht von Scharfenberg
c.1300	The Didot Perceval (Didot was MS owner)	Anonymous
c.1315	The Elucidation (prologue to the Grail story)	Anonymous
1325-1400	Peredur (a much earlier story included in the "Mabinogian" of these dates. The Welsh Perceval)	Anonymous
1485	Le Morte d'Arthur (based maily on Vulgate cycle; general merging of Round table romances and Grail myth)	Thomas Malory
1856-1859 & 1868-74	Idylls of the King	Alfred Lord Tennyson
1850	The opera "Lohengrin"	Richard Wagener
1882	The opera "Parsifal"	Richard Wagener

Appendix 3

The Mountain of the Philosophers
An Interpretation of the Initiate's journey

Abstract of the Article Published in the Rosicrucian Digest No, 3,1995.
By Art Kompolt F.R.C.

Historical Perspective

The philosophical and esoteric ideas expressed in "The Mountain of the Philosophers" come from the Western Hermetic and Alchemical esoteric traditions. The symbols used in the engraving present a visual touchstone similar to that of archetypes studied and explained by the psychologist Carl G. Jung.

Paul Diel also describes the universality of symbolical language, and explains that its psychological significance is found abundantly in the Bible. Diel says, "The symbols created by the super conscious imagination can in no way exist outside of the inner psychic life." This means that deciphering symbolic language can only be accomplished through an introspective method.

One of the purposes of "The Mountain of the Philosophers" engraving is its use as a mandala. A mandala, of course, is a drawing that is used as a guide for contemplation and spiritual exercises. In his work "The Alchemical Mandala," Adam Mclean provides a survey of forty engravings with commentaries in the Western Esoteric Tradition.

Descriptive Interpretation of the Plate

A description of the symbols found in "The Mountain of the Philosophers" provides us with a road map to initiation and the Grail. Let us examine the plate in more detail and try to interpret some of the many symbols found within the illustration.

We begin toward the bottom of the plate where we see that the mountain is surrounded by a brick or stone wall which features an arched entrance. The entrance is guarded by a naked old man sitting on the trunk of a dead tree. He sits inside a cave and looks toward the person on the right. Symbolically, the round, brick wall provides a strong protective barrier. The round wall can also be interpreted as being part of an alchemical furnace, or the allegorical flask of the philosopher. The arched entrance is the Portal of Initiation. The bearded old man signifies the guardian of the threshold, the guardian of secrets, the terror of the threshold, the terror of death and karma, or in other words, the gatekeeper.

Three persons outside the brick wall approach the Portal of Initiation. One of the persons on the left is blindfolded and is groping to find the entrance — signifying that this person is searching outwardly and not within his inner self. Next to this blindfolded person, another person, possibly a woman, rests with her right knee on the ground due to a heavy purse. She seems to be wearing a large feather plume in her hat which covers her eyes. She looks down toward the rocks, giving the impression that she is interested in mundane, materialistic pursuits. It is obvious that the two persons on the left will not find their way to the Portal of Initiation.

On the right side of the illustration a third person actively indicates with open arms his desire to advance toward the entrance to the Portal of Initiation. In the forefront of the engraving a rabbit lurches from its burrow toward the third person. The rabbit is also easily frightened and to the uninitiated signifies fleeting thoughts. It is necessary for the initiate to have quietude in the quest.

The year 1604 appears in large numbers near the rabbit. According to the *Confessio Fraternitatis*, the legendary Christian Rosenkreutz was born in 1378 and died in 1484 at 106 years of age. His grave was said to have been opened in 1604 —120 years after his death — and his body was perfectly preserved. This date provides us with an important episode in the history of the Rosicrucian tradition — the rediscovery of the body of ancient esoteric knowledge by Rosicrucian brethren and the reopening of Rosicrucian activities in Europe.

The old man sits at the portal and guards the entrance to a cave leading into "The Mountain of the Philosophers." The cave symbolises a place of gloom, but

1604

also a place of initiation and integration. It also signifies the Alchemy which is at work in the interior of the earth.

In order to pass through the portal, a person must satisfy the gatekeeper — the guardian of the threshold — and follow the passage into the unknown mountain. This is the initiate's first test.

The Path to the Grail

The path to the Grail is seen to spiral up the side of the mountain. To the left of the guardian, above the wall and near archway, there is pictured another rabbit, which looks similar to the rabbit outside the walls. On the opposite side of the archway we find a brooding hen on a nest of eggs signifying the warmth, willpower, and tenacity necessary for the development of imagination, so that thoughts become external objects — an important step as the initiate ascends the mountain.

The rabbit and brooding hen are symbols describing the alchemical process of inner transformation. The rabbit works with its quick and dynamic energies, while the hen portrays the carefully slow meditation process, sometimes known as active imagination. Both these energies and processes must be activated by the initiate in order to pass the second test.

Upon success, the initiate can proceed through the inner darkness of the cave and upwards towards the left to where the passage emerges into the light above a rocky ridge guarded by a fiery dragon. The dragon symbolises the primal unresolved energies of the unconscious, along with the unleashed instincts, impulses, and desires which the initiate must fight and conquer through the will power.

When the initiate successfully works through the process and gains control of his or her psychic energies, he or she will have then passed the inner test and can stand in the centre of the mountain where they face yet another test.

At the centre of the mountain the initiate faces a third guardian — a golden, proud lion blocks the path. The lion is a manifestation of human feelings, pleasures, and aversions. This symbol is a reflection of egoism and false spiritual pride. It is very important that the initiate recognise this false spiritual pride, and be strong and guard against it.

Upon successful completion of this test the initiate can enter through a second portal (seen in the centre of the mountain) which leads into an inner citadel. Here the initiate meets a black crow and a white eagle. These are the "soulbirds" which can help the initiate experience various manifestations of the unconscious. The black crow is a stage in alchemy known as nigredo, which portrays the blackening and dark experiences of the unconscious. The white eagle signifies the lofty heights of spirit analogous to the raising of vapours during distillation.

To the left of the citadel tower we see the Sun and Moon — the two polarities —in a wooden tub, symbolising the purification of the initiate's solar and lunar characteristics. Purification and washing of the dross accumulations within our soul is done through use of water.

To the right of the citadel tower we see a flask within a furnace. The flask represents the philosopher. Inner purification takes place through the process of fire, which is accomplished through distillation in a fiery furnace. Upon completion of the purification processes, the initiate can pass through the entrance to the citadel and stand within its inner court.

Towards the top of the citadel (on the left) the initiate encounters an old man holding a tree with its roots dangling above the wooden tub which holds the Sun and Moon. The old man is planting a tree in the tub where the Sun and Moon — the polarities — have been purified. The tree's roots seem to be drawing upon the Sun and Moon's energies and thus producing a living tree with a seven-pointed star and a flask of fruits. The seven-pointed star signifies the essence of the planetary forces, and the flask is the vessel where these forces can be manifested.

On the right side of the citadel, high above the furnace, is a tree bare of foliage with three six-pointed stars. The tree leans toward the smoke rising from the distillation furnace. The three stars adoring the tree signify the alchemical principals: salt, sulphur, and mercury.

On the citadel's rocky heights there is a house with smoke rising from its chimney. This is the house of the holy spirit where the soul of the initiate can find shelter and awareness of the spiritual. This is the temple where subtle alchemical changes take place when the spirit, soul and body are brought into harmony and balance.

At the peak of the rocky heights is an orb topped with a cross which is the sign for VITRIOL — an anagram which is interpreted to mean "Visit the interior of the earth and by purifying, there discover the hidden stone."

The initiate who undertakes the inner journey and has achieved the orb gains a crown signifying spiritual attainment and cosmic illumination. The crown hovers above the mountain peak.

Above the mountain, the Sun and Moon are seen released from their three-dimensional enslavement. The Sun and the Crescent moon, correctly oriented in the sky, are the signs of the Grail, and symbolic of Cosmic Illumination.

Bibliography

ACHAD, Frater, **The Chalice of Ecstasy, Parzival,** Yogi P.S., Chicago, 1973.

ANDREAS, P.,& Davies, R.l., **Das Verheimliche Wissen,** Ansata, München, 1984

ASHE, G., **Camelot and the Vision of Albion,** Heinemann, London, 1981.

ASHE, G., **King Arthur's Avalon: The Story of Glastonbury,** Fontana, G.B., 1957

ASHE, G., **The Landscape of King Arthur,** Grange, London, 1987.

ASHLEY, M., **The Merlin Cronicles,** Raven Books, London, 1995.

BAIGENT, M., et al., **Holy Blood and the Holy Grail,** Corgi, London, 1987.

BECK A., **Der Untergang der Templer,** Heder, Freiburg, 1992.

BEGG, E. and D. **In Search of the Holy Grail and the Precious Blood,** Thorstens, London, 1995.

BERNADAC, C., **Montségur et le Graal,** France-Empire, Paris, 1994

BLUM, J., **Mystère et Messages des Cathares,** Le Rocher, France, 1989.

BOLEN, J.S., **Crossing to Avalon,** Harper, San Francisco, 1994.

BRYCE, D., **The Mystical Way and the Arthurian Quest,** Dyfed, Wales, 1986

CAMPBELL, J., (ed.), **The Mysteries,** Vol. 2, Princeton, NJ, 1855.

CAMPBELL, J., **Transformations of Myth through Time,** Harper and Row, New York, 1987.

CARR-GOMM, P., **The Druid Tradition,** Element, G.B. 1993.

CAVENDISH, R., **King Arthur and the Grail,** Weidenfeld and Nicholson, London, 1978.

CHARPENTIER, L., **Les Mystères de la Cathédrale de Chartres,** Laffont, Paris, 1966.

COGLAN, R., **The Illustrated Encyclopaedia of Arthurian Legends,** Element, G.B., 1993

de SORVAL, G., **La voie chevaleresque et l'initiation royale dans la tradition chrétienne,** Dervy, Panis, 1993.

DIETZFELBINGER, K., **Mysterienschulen,** Eugen Diederichs Verlag, München, 1997.

DUVAL, P., **La Pensée Alchimique et Le Conte du Graal,** Champion, Paris 1979.

ELIADE, M., **Rites and Symbols of Initiation,** Harper and Row, New York, 1958.

ELLIS, P.B., **Dictionary of Celtic Mythology,** ABC-CLIO, California, 1992.

EVOLA, J., **The Mystery of the Grail** (trans. Stucco G.) Inner Traditions, Rochester, Vermont, 1997.

FANTHOME, L., and P., **Secrets of Rennes le Château,** Weiser, Maine, 1992.

FIEBAG, J., and P., **Die Entdeckung des Grals,** Goldman, München, 1989.

FROMM, E., **Escape from Freedom,** Avon Books, New York., 1965.

GADAL, A., **Das Erbe der Katharer und Das Druidentum,** Rosenkruis Pers, Haarlem, Holland, 1993.
GADAL, A., **Montréalp de Sos,** Rosenkruis Pers, Haarlem, Holland, 1981.
GODWIN, M., **The Holy Grail,** Bloombury, London, 1994.
GOODRICH, N. L., **The Holy Grail,** Harper Collins, NY, 1992
GREEN, M., **Celtic Myths,** British Museum, London, 1993.
GREEN, M., **Dictionary of Celtic History and Legend,** London, 1992.
HADINGTON, E., **Circles and Standing Stones,** Abacus, London, 1978.
HARRISON, H., **The Cauldron and the Grail,** Archives Press, California, 1992.
HELENE, C., **Mysteries of the Holy Grail,** New Age, Los Angeles, 1977.
HOWARTH, S., **The Knights Templar,** Dorset, New York, 1982.
JOHNSON, K. & Elsbeth M., **The Grail Castle,** Llewellyn, St. Paul, MI 1995.
JOHNSON, K., **Interview in New Worlds,** July—August 1997.
JOHNSON, R., **The Fisher King and the Handless Maiden,** Harper Collins, NY, 1993.
JUNG, E., and von Franz, M.L., **The Grail Legend,** Sigo, Boston, 1986
KNIGHT, G., **The Secret Tradition in Arthurian Legend,** Aquarian, Wellingborough, U.K., 1983.
LAVENU, P., **L'ésotérisme du Graal,** Tredanniel, Paris, 1989.
LOOMIS, R. S., **Celtic Myth and Arthurian Romance,** Constable, London, 1993.
LOOMIS, R. S., **The Grail. from Celtic Myth to Christian Symbol,** Constable, London, 1993
LOOMIS, R. S., **Wales and the Arthurian Legend,** Cardiff, 1956.
MACKIE, E., **The Megalith Builders,** Phaedon, Oxford, 1977.
MARKALE, J., **Brocéliande et L'énigme du Graal,** Pygmalion, Paris, 1989.
MARKALE, J., **Chartres et L'énigme des Druides,** Pygmalion, Paris, 1988.
MARKALE, J., **Gisors, et L'énigme de Templiers,** Pygmalion, Paris, 1986.
MARKALE, J., **Le cycle du Graal, Les Chevaliers de la Table Ronde,** Pygmalion, Paris, 1993.
MARKALE, J., **Women of the Celts** (translates by Mygind, Hauch and Henry), Cremonesi, London, 1975
MASLOW, A., **Towards a Psychology of Being,** Litton, NY, 1968
MATARASSO, P. M., **The Quest of the Holy Grail,** Penguin, London, 1969.
MATTHEWS, C, and J., **Ladies of the Lake,** Harper and Collins, London, 1992.
MATTHEWS, J., **The Arthurian Tradition,** Element, G.B., 1989.
MATTHEWS,J., **The Grail, Quest for the Eternal,** Thames & Hudson, 1981.
MATTHEWS, J. (ed), **At the Table of the Grail,** Arkana, London, 1987.

MATTHEWS, J. (ed), **Household of the Grail,** Aquarian, U.K., 1990.
MATTHEWS,J., **The Arthurian Reader,** Harper Collins, London, 1991.
MATMEWS, J., **The Grail Tradition,** Element, Shaftesbury, 1983.
MEADEN, G. T., **The Goddess of the Stones,** Souvenir London, 1991.
MILLER, R.,& I., **The Modern Alchemist,** Phanes, Grand Rapids, Michigan, 1994.
NEUMANN, E., **The Great Mother,** (transl) R. Matinheim), Princeton, NY, 1972.
OWELLY, C., **Newgrange,** Wexford, Ireland, 1978.
PARTNER, R, **The Knights Templar and Their Myth,** Destiny, Rochester Vermont 1990.
PEDERSEN, L. E., **Dark Hearts,** Shamballa, London, 1991.
PONSOIE, P., **Islam et le Graal,** Arche, Milan, Italy, 1976.
RAVENSCROFT, T., **The Cup of Destiny,** Weiser, Maine, 1982.
RAVENSCROFT, T., **The Spear of Destiny,** Weiser, Maine, 1985.
REGNIER-Bohler, D., (Directeur), **La Légende Arthurienne,** Laffont, Paris, 1989.
RIZNIKOV, R., **Cathares et Templiers,** Loubatières, Toulouse, 1993.
ROBERTS, I. F, **Symbols of the Grail Quest,** Spirit of Celtia, Weymouth, 1990.
ROHR, R., **Quest for the Grail,** Crossroad, NY, 1994.
ROLLESTON, W. T., **Celtic Myths and Legends,** Gresham, London, 1994.
SAMSONETTI, R.G., **Graal et Alchimie,** Berg International, Paris, 1982.
SHARKEY, J., **Celtic Mysteries,** Thames and Hudson, London, 1975.
SINCLAIR, A., **The Sword and the Grail,** Random House, London, 1994.
SKLAR, D., **The Nazis and the Occult,** Dorset, NY, 1977.
SPENCE, L., **The Mysteries of Britain,** Mckay, Philadelphia, 1972. (reprint by Health Research).
von dem Borne, G., **The Gral in Europa,** Fisher, Stuttgart, 1987.
WAITE, A. E.,**The Hidden Church of the Holy Grail,** London, 1909. (reprint, Yogi, de Planes, Illinois -undated)
WAITE, A. E., **The Holy Grail: Legends and Symbolism,** NY, 1961.
WALSHE, R. N., and Vaughan, F, (ed.) **Beyond Ego,** Tarcher, Los Angeles, 1980.
WESTON, J. L., **From Ritual to Romance,** Princeton, NJ, 1993.
WHITMONT, E. C., **Return of the Goddess,** Arkana, London, 1987.
WIELAND, F., **The Journey of the Hero,** Prism, Bn'dport, 1991.
WILMSHURST, W.L., **Parsifal,** Sure Fire Press, Edmonds, WA, USA, 1993.
WRIGHT, D., **Druidism, the Ancient Faith of Britain,** E. P. Publishing, U.K., 1976.

Index

A

Abred, 98
Aberrystwyth, 12
Achad, Frater, 81
Adam, and Fall of Man, 83,99,122
Adulteress, Guinevere as, 122
Albi, 12
Albigensian Crusade, 13,24,25,30-1
Albrecht von Scharfenberg, 23,34,46,136
Alchemical Wedding, 52,53
Alchemists as sorcerers. 40
Alchemy, and Arabs, 39; Grail and symbols in,48; process in, 48,63; continues mystery tradition, 46,47; crowned king symbol in, 63; Grail in, Ch.6; nigredo phase,16, 48,49,63; nature and practice of,40,46, 47; transcendental, 47; transmutation in, 48,126; Wedding symbol in, 51,52; Wolfram and, 115
Allegory, 40,50
Amangons, 65,123
Amfortas; 64,80,82,83,115,123;as fallen Man, 115
American Occupation Forces, 82
Amide, Perceval's sister, 106
Ancestry, 114
Anima, 57,58,59,77; see also "Feminine Principle"
Animus/Anima, 56,60,72,77; in harmony, 59,72,77,90,119
Angels, 15,53
Annihilation,105
Annwn, Arthur's descent to, 98
Antioch, 81
Apostolic succession, 68
Aprentice column, 32
Arabs and alchemy, 39
Aragon, 38
Ark of the Covenant, 48
Archeology, 74
Archetypes, Archetypal energies:*animus, anima,* 57,58,59,77,82; energies of the unconscious, 121; interplay of, 60; language of the unconscious 58; of Grail Quest, 94; persona, 58,59; repression of shadow, 58; self as integrator, 56,101; wise man,51,62
Architecture in Spain, 40
Ariège, 121
Art and Architecture, 39,40
Arimathea, Joseph of: see "Joseph".
Arnaud, M., 30
Arrows, Pass of the, 32
Arthur, King, 28,33,106,110,122,128; Avalon and, 33; Arthunian locations in Wales, 32; Arthurian tales, 76; Cross of, 33; descent to Annwn, 98; failure to hold Round Table together, 123; Knights of, 54,57,116; Lady of the Lake and, 126; sword of, 127
Ashcroft-Nowicki, D., 107
Asheley, M., 69,80
Attis/Adonis Mysteries, 96
Authentically, Living, 118
Avalon, 33,108
Avebury Stones, 73
Axis mundi, 127

B

Babylon, Rituals of, 91
Baigent M., et. al., 26
Balearic Islands, 38
Balkans, 70
Baphomet, 93
Barcelona, 31; Bard(s), 98
Becoming, Everything is, 103
Beyond identity, 105
Birds as degree symbols, 43,92
Black Brotherhood, 83
Black Grail? 84,86

Black Knights, 61,85
Black Virgin cult, 40
Blanchefleur (White Flower), 74,76,118
Bleeding Lance, see "Spear".
Blood, Dindraine's, 126
Blood, of Christ, healing blood and magic fluid, 127; in bloodline theory, 83,115; in Chalice Well water, 108; on snow, 89,127; on spear of Longinus, 81,97
Bloodline theory: 115; family heritage and,115; Hitler's racial,83; spiritual interpretation, 115
Bolen, J.,66,119
Book(s): Corpus Hermeticum, 48; Grail as a,11,113; of Lambsprink 49,63; list of Grail texts, see Appendix 2
Bors, Bohors, Sir, 7,36,105,132
Boyne complex, Ireland, 88
Brabant, 136
Brahma, Castle of, 36
Brahman, 105
Bran, Welsh god,decapitated head of,94
Bron, Grail King,32,63,113,121
Brotherhood of Darkness, 85-6
Brotherhood of the Grail, 83-85, 133
Bruce, D., on the Templars, 22
Bubonic plague, 68
Buddahood, 104
Buddhism, 63
Buddhist, Grail imagery,111; psychology, 104
Byzantine Empire, 38

C

Cabbalists, 24,39,40
Cadwallader, King, 68
Callanish Stones, 73
Camelot, 42
Camlann, 33
Castell Dinas Bran, 32,113
Castile, 38
Catastrophe, ends Golden Age, 69-70
Cathars: 28,40,92; and Grail,93 ; and Manichaeism, 40; and seven transmgrations, 92; annihilation of, 40; celibacy of some, 93; *Credentes,* 26,92; cross, 73; fortress of Monségur, 19. influence on Grail literature, 124; in south of France, 25; Perfecti, 92; Templars, Rosicrucians and, 25; rites, 30; symbolism, 28; vegetarian habits. 92; women accorded equal status among 124
Cathedrals, 47
"Cauldron and the Grail, The", 12
Cauldron: of plenty, 32,111; magic, 98,125
Cause and Effect, Law of, 102
Caves, 111
Celestial Man, 28
Celtic: background of Grail Myth, 32,96, 113; Christianity, 68,80,113; crosses, 73; mystery tradition, 111; myths, see "Keridwen"; queens, 122; tradition of human head, 93; view of events, 67-8
Celto Roman religious conflict, 68,80
Centre of Being, 121
Ceridwen: see "Keridwen"
Ceugant, 98
Chalice Well: description of, 108; at Glastonbury, 12,33,107-8; cover, 108; Rosicrucians at, 108
Chandhogya Upanishad, 36
Charlemagne, 38
Chartres Cathedral, 37,47
Chetwynd, 56
Circle of Happiness, 98
Chivalry, 18,39,106,114
Chrétien de Troyes, 6,10,15,113,116,122, 129,185; his *Le Conte del Graal,* 18,19, 112,116,122,129,135
Christ: 41; appears before hermit,11; blood of, 26,127; consciousness, 105; see also "Jesus"
Christian: fish and Christian symbol, 63; Europe, 38; Moslem, Jew and, 40; in

mystery 75,124,125; symbolism. 125; view of events, 25-7
Christ's blood, 26,127
Christianity,Orthodox& Grail, 113,134
Church of Rome, 69; and heretics, 40, 41; and Celtic Christianity, 68,80, 113; as central authority, 38; attitudes towards Grail, 40; exoteric teaching, 44; leads Crusades, 38; views of salvation, 40
Circles, Overlap of two, 119
Cistercian Order, 41,69,132,135; and Vulgate cycle, 40
Compassion, Developing, 106,118-9
Condwiramur, 118,127; see also "Blanchefleur"
Consolamentum, 30,93
Cookhouse, 51
Continuations of *Le Conte del Graal* 129, 135; Gawain in, 129
Corbenic, Grail Castle, 121
Corpus Hermeticum, 48
Corsica, 38
Cosmic Consciousness:see "Consciousness"
Consciousness; Christ, 115; raising level of 118; shift in, 120; spectrum of, 115,116
Cosmic mind and self, 105
Courtly love, 40
Credentes, 26,92
Crown: Diû Krône, 11,122,136; initiatic degree in mysteries, 41; Lucifer's 113
Crowned King, Symbol of, 49,63
Crucifixion and Mary, 75
Crusade(s), against the Grail, 31; against Islam, 22,39; Albigensian, 13, 19,30-1; benefits of, 39; First 39; influences of islam on, 38; Spear discovered during, 81
Cup, Grail as a; at Caldy island, 12; at Glastonbury, 12; in Rosslyn Chapel, 32; in statue at Chartres, 27; as maintainer of life, 27; Nanteos, 12
Cyclic nature, 9,63-4

D

Dames, M., 96
Dark Ages, Britain in, 68
"Dark Night": see "nigredo"
Dark Side: in Klingsor, 80-1; of the Grail Myth, 79; in Red Knight, 57
Darwin, law of survival, 83
Debate on nature of the Grail, 14
De Boron see "Robert de Boron"
De Hauteville, Roger, 38
Dee, River, 32
Degenerate Man, 1122
Degrees of Initiation: see "Initiation"
Degrees of Instruction, 42
de Meung, Lorris and, 51-52
Demonic powers, 83-4
Demonstration of courtly virtues, 118
Der Junge Titurel, 120,136
Der Jungere Titurel, 46,120,136
Destiny and the Individual, 121
Devouring female, 77
Didot Perceval, 113,136
Castell Dinas Bran, 32,113
Dindraine, Story of, 106; see "Amide"
Discrimination in judgement, 127
Diû Krône, 11,122,136
Divine Will, 85
Dolorous Stroke, 126
"Doors of Perception", 49
Double intent of Grail romances, 41,91, 92,94
Dove, 51,112,135
Dowth Tumulus, 88
Dragon Symbol, 51
Druidic mysteries, 96-7,111
Drops of blood or fluid, 98
Dualism, 85
Dustbin, 51

E

Early societies, Feminine principle in, 72-3
Earth, Caring for the, 102
Earth energies, 19
Earth Goddess, 70,72,73, 89,111,128
Effort and endeavour, 42
Ego, 50,66,67; as discriminator, 60; beyond, 104-5; control, 58; death of ego, 44; journey of the, 104; management by, 58; over identification with, 58; sacrifice or enhancement of, 93,101
Egyptian, counterpart of Grail, 111; initiatic degree of, 41
Eisenhower, General, 82
Eleanor d'Aquitaine, 73
Eleusis, Ritual bowl at, 74
Elite, under Hitler, 83-4
Elucidation, The, 65,123,125,134
Enlightenment, 42,104-6,131
Enchantment, 99
Environment, Caring for the, 102
Escape from Freedom, Erich Fromm's, 99
Esclarmonde de Foix, 73
Esoteric character of Grail Christianity, 40
Esoteric intent, 91
Eucharist, 89,96,124
Europe, State of, 99; beliefs in Medieval, 90; rituals in. 90
Evola, J., 77
Evolvement of Man, 115
Exile, State of, 98-9
Experience in Otherworld, 120
Exoteric intent, 40,91
Extreme health, 104-5
Eye of Horus, 19,48

F

Fall and Redemption, 44,64,98
Father figure, 63.64,92117,118
Feeling function, 66
Female figurines, 97
Female knight? 77
Feminine principle: 56,57,67, 72,124; acknowledged by Cathars, 124; and disharmony with masculine principle, 67; and unconscious, 116; as mediator, 122; aspects of, 128-9; in Black Knight episode, 60; in Kundry, 128; in Grail Queen, 64,122; in Grail Maiden, 59; in Lady in the Tent, 53; in Sophia, 74 ; in Maidens of the Wells, 65; in Gnosticism, 39; in secret of the Grail, 125
Firefiz, 18,48,50
First Continuation, 135
Fish, as symbol, 63,64,119
Fisher King. see "Grail King"
Fisherman, Peter the, 63; Grail King Bran as, 63; role of, 63-4
"Fishers of Men", 63
Fishing, 64; as symbol, 119
Fool, Perceval as a, 53,56, 66-7, 106
Forces of Light and Darkness, 129
Forest as symbol, 56,115,116
Fourth Continuation, 135
Freemasons, 32
Free Will, 42,68,70
Franks, 38
Fromm, E, 99
Frontier of conscious and unconscious, 120
Fulfilment, Striving for, 77

G

Gahmuret, in Arabia, 18
Galahad, 4,6,36,69,105,110,114, 123,127, 131,132; a Christian hero, 69,98,123; and Jesus, 42; and Sarras; 29,123; and sword, 127; as cardboard figure, 132; compared with Perceval, 42, 110,132; finds the Grail, 105; in the *Queste*, 113-4,132; ascends to heaven,

29, 123,132; sits in Perilous Seat, 114,123; united with God, 123
Gawain (Gwalchmai), 32,36,50, 106, 111, 121, 128, 129
Glastonbury, Abbey at, 33,113,122; Arthur's grave at, 33; as home of the Grail, 113-4; as pagan site, 113; Chalice Well House at, 33; cup, 12; Henry VIII and, 12,33; "Isle of Glass", 33; is mystic Avalon, 108; Rosicrucian visit to, 108; thorn, 33; Tor, 33; Wearyall Hill, 33; Zodiac, 114
Gender Specificity,72, 108
Gerald of Wales, 33
Gerbert de Montreuil, 135, 135
Gestapo, 103
Goddess: see also "Earth Goddess", "Feminine Principle", "Women"; and Grail, 125; and archaeology, 74-5; as tester and guide, 128; as theme in Grail myth, Ch. 9; cosmic aspects of, 77 ; in Avebury Stones, 73; negative and positive aspects, 128-9; subservience to male god, 72-3; womb of, 72-4; the world as female, 76
Gnosis, secret, 94
God, Quest as return to, 76
Godwin, M, 16,40,65
Gold, in Grail Quest, 63; Alchemy, 48, 63,130
Golden Age: see "Paradise"
Good and Evil, 115,129
Good Friday, 113
Gournemanz, 54,58,118,129,132
Gradale, 112
Grace of God, 41,66,120
Greater Self, 105
Greece, Rituals of, 91

Grail, and Cathars, 13; and Emerald Tablet, 19; and Eucharist, 11,15; and Horus, 19; and Lia Fail, 19; and Mary Magdalene, 31; and philosophers' stone, 16; and pineal gland, 19; answering the call of the, 71,89; as a book, 11; as a cask containing bread, 11; as a cup or chalice, 11, 12, 16, 81, 87, 98,112,124,126; as a cup of wisdom, 98; as a cup in Rosslyn Chapel, 32; as containing divine redeeming substance, 87; as female symbol, 76; as fertility symbol, 96; gives spiritual nourishment 107; as a head on plate, 16,111; as healer, 76, 131; as horn of plenty, 111; as quest for femininity, 76; as the Greater Self, 62; as a jewel, 35; as an idea of relationship,13; as a message in architecture or sculpture 32; as a memory of Paradise, 98; as a miraculous object, Ch. 1., 127; as myth, 9,98; as point of reconciliation, 44; as a physical object, 11,13,15; as a relic, 15; as restorer of wasteland, 75; as a sacred or mystical object, 111; as shape-shifter, 11; as spirit, 59; as a stone 15,16,47,125; as a storehouse of wisdom, 11; as a symbol, 13,44,76,93; as a *vesica piscis* experience, 109; at Arthur's Court, 129; at Glastonbury, 108; banquet, 96, 124; becomes "holy", 112; being called to the, 116; Being the, 104; Brotherhood of the, 82; call of the, 120; causes fertility, 65; cautions against revealing: secrets, 125; Christianity and the, 39,42; Christianisation of,10,15,112; Christians origins of, 112; description in *Le Conte del Graal* 10,112; description in Malory's work, 106; degree of experience of the Grail, 105; description of, 112; drinking contents of, 104, 105; final vision of, 103; gives nourishment, 107; imparts immortality, 15; in

Chartres Cathedral, 27; in creative process, 81; home of the, see "Grail Castle", "Grail Kingdom"; lance and, 75; locations of the Grail, 12,13,29, 31; magical qualities of the , 10; in mystery, Ch. 6; mystery and mystic nature of, 11,124; "of the heart", 118; "peak" experience and , 104; power of the, 44; Perceval's first experience of, 57; pre Christian, 15; proto Grail, 89; secrets, 76.126; seeing the, 104; seen in Dindraine, 107; spiritual origins of, 25; taken to Heaven, 132; transformative power of, 10; uncovering the, 132; spiritual change, 71; visit to the Round Table, 106; visit to Rosenkrcutz's hut, 52; women as bearers of, 121
Grail Bearer, see "Grail Maiden"
Grail Castle or Temple, 29,76,93,102, 103,131; another dimension of human experience, 120; a prototype of mandala, 35; as Corbenic, 120; as cosmic mirror, 35; as macrocosm, 19; as Otherworldly symbol, 59,121; as the unconscious, 57, 120; described in *Parzival* 29,48; difficult access to 29; Dinas Bran, 113; early development in Star Temples, 84,111; Grail kept in, 104; in *Der Junge Titurel*, 20,120; in *Der Jungere Titurel*, 23, 34; in theHoly Land, 27; in the Middle East, 111; in "Other world", 120; in theMons Philosophorum, 50-1; in sacred caves, 111; in the *Queste*, 19, 31; in *Sone of Nansai*, 120; the Interior Castle, 27,121; meeting point of Heaven and Earth, 121; Montségur as, 13,18,31; Montsalvaesche, Montsalvat 9, 16; Montserrat, 5, 9, 18; Himmler's, 85; off Norway's coast, 120; as "peak" experience, 104; Perceval's visit to,93,98,130; pre historic thought form of, 35; prototype of the, 34; Pyrenean fortress, 114; resembled Templar fortress, 114; resembled Holy Sepulchre, 23; Rosicrucian imagery in, 17; Rosslyn Chapel, 32; state of transcendence, 102; symbolizes sun, 102; symbol of life process, 125; topped by Holy Rose, 18; "Throne of Arches", 34; visit of Perceval to, 106,131
Grail Christianity, 40,131
Grail Experience, 88
Grail Family, Guardians, Knights: a secret society, 21; a spiritual host, 21, 133; as Cathars, 30-1; as an elite, 84; as a hierarchy of souls, 133; as "holy",112; as Templars, 21,29,43, 114; as temporal, spiritual rulers, 27; attributes of, 21,114; bloodline or legendary lineage, 21,111; Brotherhood of the Grail, 85,132; ideal to be reached, 27; in de Boron's Joseph of Arimathea, 21; in the *Queste*, 21; in the *Perlesvaus*, 21; in Parzival, 21; like a shamanic caste, 92; mythical, historical figures, 27; Order founded by Joseph, 114; symbolic lineage, 25, 26; We are Grail Guardians, 88
Grail King, Fisher King, Sick or Wounded or Maimed King: 27,32,41,48,Ch.8, 81,83,88,89,97,98,104,112. 119,120, 122,127131;Ailment of the Age, 65, 121;and fertility of land, 122; and Waste Land, Ch.8;Arthur as an example of,123-4;as father figure,63,64;as fisherman, 63,64,119; as God,102; as perfect, original Man,122; as potential Grail Knight, 98; as a symbol of lost sovereignty 98, as two persons, 121; death

of, 123; failure of, 63,64,65; in story of Fall and Redemption, 84,119-20; became selfish, 84; breaking of taboos, 123; Bran, Bron, 32,63,112; causes of illness,27; conceptions of the Grail writers on, 27; Dolorous Stroke, 126; explanations for his condition, 63,83,98,122; fishing to find a cure,117; healing the wound of, 112; in alchemy, 50.62; in Wagner's *Parsifal*, 83; kept alive by Grail, 113; King/Land nexus, 62,65,66,111, 121-2; lessons of this myth, 102 lineage in Parzival, 114; mix of Celtic and Christian beliefs, 27; qualifications of, 62; record of vegetation ritual, 92; reference in Silbury Hill, 96; responsibility of, 67; Rohr's comment, 66; rulers over an invisible Brotherhood, 23; suffers from corrupted blood; 83; suffers enchantment, 83; symbol of human condition, 70; symbol of lost sover-eignty or exile, 98,119; symbol of split with nature,122-3; weak willed, 122, wound healed by Galahad, 81, 123; wound healed in us too, 67; Wagner's opera and, 80.83

Grail Kingdom, 83,89,127,129; as the unconscious, 59; description of territory, 29; Glastonbury; 33; in Otherworld, 120; in Persia, 34; presence of God in Creation, 103; seen in alchemy, 123 transformative character, 29; various places, 29; wisdom and revelation in, 125

Grail Literature: See also individual authors in Appendix II; and Celtic Church,80; and Vulgate Cycle, 41; as nostalgia for Golden Age, 69; astrology in, 62; Catharistic nature of, 18; chivalric content of, 6; double meaning in content of. 41,93; Grail Myth and Arthurian Tradition, 40, 47; Hermetic content, 113; high point of, 15, 47; in alchemy, 50,52; initiatory character of, 98; & link with mystical tradition, 40,47, oriental influence in, 40,113; pagan elements in, 40; poets of, 40; underlying philosophy of, 41

Grail Maiden, 59,74,79,96,112,123,124

Grail Mesenger, 107; See also, "Grail Maiden", "Kundry".

Grail Myth: an echo of lost Paradise, 69,70; as female myth, 75; as part of unconscious, 68,70; a vegetation myth, 66; back-ground to the, 111; Celtic origins of, 15; counter to "dark side" 9; crucial message of the, 133; cyclic character of the, 9; "dark side of the, 81; didactic aspect, 47; oriental origins of, 15, 34; separation theme in, 98; surfaces from the unconscious, 69; the true Grail Quest, 19; transformative power, 42; women's role in ,76

Grail Mythology, 123

Grail Operas, 44

Grail Procession, 59,75,81,111,123-4;

GrailQueen, 50,76,120,121-2

GrailQuest: a journey of Rosenkreutz, 351-2; a return to God, 46-76; early forms of,90; individual and collective aspect 41,107,108; journey of the soul, 36; like Arthur's descent to Annwn,98; male hero's outward quest,76; myth of return, 98; questers are chosen, 29-30; precursors of the, 111;search for philosophers' stone, 48,63; seven chambers of transition,36; shaping of the, Appendix I; start of, 106,107; success or failure in, 36; symbols in, 41; to the centre of one's being, 46; transformative value of, 48

Grail Secret: a mystery, 124,125; conjecture as to nature of, 125; given by

Jesus to Joseph, 23; one of transformation, 102; partial enlightenment, 59; passed on to Joseph's successors, 23; shown to Galahad, 132; the mean-ing of life creation, 125
Grail Tradition, and Rosicrucian 13; in Grail poetry and the Mysteries, 41,47; Matthews, J., and the, 85; practised in secret, 40
Grand Saint Graal 11,114,136
"Great Tradition", 93,102
Greater Mysteries:See"Higher mysteries"
Greater Self, 104
Greece, 91
Gwalchmai: See "Gawain"
Guinevere, 33,76,111,121,122
Gwion, 98,127
Gwynvydd, 98

H

Hall, M., 92,93
Hansend,77
Hapsburg Museum, 79,82
Harmony, State of, 131
Hare, symbol of, 52,139
Harrison, H., 12,19,42,87
Health: 100,104
Healing:102; hero as healer, 12; our wounds,72; psychic harmony and, 46; psychologist's view of, 103 splitsin psyche and, 58
Heat process in alchemy, 125
Heinrich von dem Türlin, 10,122
Helinandus, Chronicle of, 112
Hen, as symbol, 52,139
Henry VIII and Glastonbury, 12,35
Heresies, 40
Hermes Trismegistos, 27,48,50
Hermetism, 39,40
Hermetic Law of Correspondence, 48
Hermeticism in Wolfram's work, 23,40,111
Hermit: See also "Trevrizent", 48,130; contrasted with monks, 130
Herzeleid ("Heart's Sorrow"), 115
Hierarchy of needs, 103
Hierophants of the Mysteries ,102,130
High History of the Grail, 11
Higher love, 119
Higher or Greater Mysteries, 89.90,95,126
Higher values, 117
Himmler, Heinrich, 31,85
Hindu counterpart of the Grail, 111
Hitler, Adolf: 78ff; and formation of elite, 81; and heroic literature, 81; and occult, 79,and Spear of Destiny, 81; as dictator, 82; armed as Grail Knight, 82; explains Fisher King's wound 82; his aberration, 84; his attachment to *Parsifal*, 80,81; interest in Wagner's operas, 82; on Grail knighthood, 82; race theory and
Guardians, 44,82
Holy City: See "Jerusalem"
Horns of Plenty, 41,111
Horus, Eye of, 19,48
Huesca, and St. Lawrence, 13
Human nature, aspects of, 103,104
Hutin, Serge, 52

I

Ideal person, 122
Idylls of the King, 46,137
Images, primordial, 56
Illumination, 104,,108,121,130
Individual: and society, 102,129; in cosmic struggle, 127; initiative, 40,41; quest, 42; responsibility, 102
Individualism, 16,103
Induction in chivalry, 117
Initiates, poets as, 93; testing of , 127
Initiatic Tradition, 11,40-1; and Templars, 21; and troubadours,41;as projection into literature,4; ceremonies at

Newgrange, 90; degrees or grades in, 93; journey of Rosenkreutz, 52; seen in Grail romances, 11; Masters of the, 44
Initiation: description of, 121
grades of, 41; into chivalry.117;
into higher mysteries, 48,89
movements and objects in, 124;
Parzival's awakening to,116;
Parzival's final, 130
second level of, 120ff; as union with God, 123
Initiatory Orders, 101-3
Integration, 48,101,103,131
Interiorization of ritual, 87
"Interior Castle" of St.Teresa, 36
Introspection, 59,127
Intuition,value of, 117
Invisible Brotherhood, 1323
Invisible world, 59,119
Islam. advance into Europe, 38; Judaism, Christianity and, 40; Knightly Orders of 16,92; Parzival themes traced to, 106
Isle of Glass, 20

J

Javelin, symbolic meaning of, 117
Jerusalem:and Crusades,39; is Sarras, 123.131; Temple of Solomon in, 76
Jesus, and Galahad compared,42; and "fishers of men", 62; and lost Paradise, 70; and Mary Magdalene, 27; and Perceval compared, 41; connection with Montserrat, 31; in priest king tradition, 27; pierced by lance, 78,81
Johnson, K., 78
Johnson, R., 66
Joseph of Arimathea, 33,112,132 and Bron, the Grail King, 32; arrival at Glastonbury,114; brings Grail to Glastonbury, 107; in de Boron's work, 11, 21,112,135; and secrets of Jesus, 22
Josephe, 12
Journey, of Rosenkreutz, 51-2; of the ego, 102; of the hero, 96,10-6; of the soul, 88
"Joust in Heaven", 47
Judas, and Perilous Seat, 113
Jung,E., and von Franz M L.,31,34
Der Junge Titurel, 136

K

Keridwen's Cauldron, 96-8,124
Kingship, 46,62
Klingsor, assisted by Kundry, 128; "dark side", 81; human will vs. divine will, 81; magic of, 119; misuse of spear, 81; 123; part played in Parzival,129,132
Knight = warrior, soldier, 92
Knight, G., 41
Knights, as Grail winners, 105; code of chivalry, 117; female, 76; Order of Grail, 109; Order of the Round Table, 42,52
Knight's Quest, 89,92
Knowth, Ireland, 90
Krater at Eleusis, 74
Kundry, 32,75,76, 119,128,129,132
Kyot de Provence, 15,16

L

Lacinus, James, 48,62
Lady in theTent, assault on, 76,116; bestowing sovereignty, 116; symbolic violation of, 76,117
Lady of the Lake, 119,126,127
Lake, as symbol of the mind, 119
Lambsprinck, Book of, 49,63-4
Lancelot, 36,44105,118,119,122

Lancelot Grail, 11
Languedoc, 18,32,40
"Lapsit exillis", 16
Last Supper, 21,103
Law of Correspondence, 48
Leadership in the Quest, 123
Le Conte del Graal: See "Chrétien"
Le Morte d'Arthur, 136
Le Roman de l'histoire du Graal:
See Robert de Boron
"Lesser Holy Grail", 112
Life force, 127
Light and darkness, 115
Liminal experiences of Bolen, 119
Lineage, 114
Lion, Initiatic Degree of, 42-3,94
Lion Headed figure, 92
Llangollen, 31
Llydaw, Lake, 19
Loathsome Creature: See "Kundry"
Logres, Land of, 65,126
Lohengrin, 114, 137
London, 94
Longinus, 79,80, 113,114
Lorris and de Meung, 51
Love, Experiencing, 118,119,126; levels of, 118,119,126; selfless, 105
Loyalty, Gawain's, 128
Lucifer. 15,48,113
Lugh, Lance of, 77,126
Luke, H., 76-7

M

"Machoism", 78
McLean, 47
Macrocosm, individual's effect on 128
Magdalenean Grail, 93
Magic, 93; weapons of, 111
Magician, as mentor,hermit, 92
Maidens of the Wells, 65,122
Male/female balance, 75,93
Male attributes/principle, 53,56,67,72, 78,92; See also "father figure"
Male god dominance, 72
Malory, Thomas, 46,136
Maltwood, K., 10,114
Manessier's Continuation, 130,135
Manichaeism, 30,39,92
Manisola rite, 30,92
Mankind, Role of, 69
Marie de Champagne, 73
Marie de France, 74
Markale, J., 25,75
Marseille, 13,31
Mary, and Christian Mystery, 75; as divine vessel, 76
Masculinity, 56,57,89
Maslow, A: "Peak,' exprience, 104,119; pyramid of needs, 103; notion of superior people,103; self-actualization, 101,103
Masters, Initiatic, 44
Matter of Britain, Ireland, 15,111
Matthews, C., 34,36,99,100
Matthews, J., 12,13,36,77,88
Megalith Builders, 34-5,111; of "Star Temples", 81
Melchisedek, 11,27,47
Men's quest, not just for femininity,78
Mental, health crisis, 58
Mercury, 48,50
Merlin, 11,27,135
Merovingian rulers, 27
Message of the Grail and Quest, 133-4
Method of Perfecting Base Metals, 48
Mind, 55,104,105,119
Minnesingers, 19,41
Mithraic cult, 92; degrees, 90
Modern mystic, 106,107
Mohammed, 38
Monasteries: and Henry VIII, 12;
Mons Philosophorum, 50, Appendix 3
Montrealp de-Sos, 513
Montsalvasche, Monsalvat, 19,29,31
Montségur, 18,30-32,92,114

Montserrat monastery, 13,18,31
Monn symbol, 39
Moral degeneration, 64,88
Mordred, 126
Morgan, 77
Morte d 'Arthur, 46
Moslem conquests in Europe, 38
Mother archetype, 53,71,115
Mother Goddess: See "Earth Goddess"
Moys,and Perilous Seat, 123
Mysteries, Mystery School Movements, Cults,39,62,90,92,93,94,96,101,121, 125,126; Christian, 62,90,125; Druidic, 96; of Keridwen ,96, Oriental, 96; purpose of Mystery Initiation, 95
Mystery School Tradition: and alchemy, 47; connection of Perlesvaus with, 11; Druidic, 96; in East, 92; in France, 18,27; link with ancients, 92,94,106; magical or sacred, 92-3; mystery content and effects, 94
Mystic consciousness, 48,52; Modern 106; path to, 44; use of intuition in,117
Mystical activity, Middle Ages, 38
Mystical approach, Western, 106
Mystical Experience, 92,105,111,121; interpreted in Parsifal, 15; view of progress, 84
Mystic message of Wagner, 132-3
Mysticism, European, 40; Sufi, 40
Myth: and history, 131; "dark side" of, 81ff; function of, 56; Grail, as healer, 40; interioration of, 84; nature of, 87,133; negative char-acter of, 87; psychological meaning in, 87 value of,101; vegetation, 67;

N

Natural grace, loss of, 12
Navarre, 31
Nazis, 31,77ff
Needs; See "Hierarchy of Needs"
Neolithic times, 96
Newgrange, 35,88; ceremonies, 35; des-cription of tumulus, 90; prototype of Grail Temple, 35; symbols at, 35
Nicodemus, Gospel of, 112
Negative forces, 127
Nigredo or "blackness" phase,or "Dark Night"; 48,60,88125,130
Nitze, H.W., 42
Noetic experience, 92
"Nordics", 121
Notre Dame Cathedrals: See "Cathedrals"
Nuremburg,St. Katherine's in, 82

O

Obligations, of man, 102; of hero,102
Onyx stone, 34
Operas: See "Wagner"
Opposites, Doctrine of, 83,102,129; unity of, 77
Oral Tradition, 111
Oriental mysteries, 96
Original sin, 67
Orthodox Christianity, 124
"Otherworld", The, 36,57,76,111,121,134
"Outremer", 16
Oversoul, 104

P

Padma mani, Buddhist, 48
Palestine, 39
Paradise or Golden Age, Concepts of 65,66,90,98; Grail literature looked

towards,60-70 ; Logres was once a, 65; on Earth, 66,69; utopia, 66,67-8
Parsi Sanctuary at Shiz, 35
Parsifal, 81,115,116,118,127,137; as renewing force, 115
Parzival, 16,18,29,40,46,48,52,65, 112, 113,114,118,122,125,128,135
Passage grave, 88-9
"Pass of the Arrows" North Wales, 32
Patriarchal organization, 72
Pelagian heresy, 67
Pelles, Grail King, 123
"Peak" experience, 104,108,119
Pelican symbol, 126
Perceval: achieves Grail, 105; and Firefiz, 18,36,40,47,50; and the Lady in the Tent, 53; and lance, 123; and self-actualization, 104; and Wounded King, 131; and swan, 69; and Wounded King, 131;as Fool, 53,54,98; as Grail King 105; as healer, 89,106, 116; as representative of mankind, 106; as symbol of Redeemer, 62,129; at Arthur's Court, 54; becomes Grail King, 55,89,131; catches lance in flight, 123, chosen to visit Grail Castle, 120,121; comes to river, 54; compared with Galahad 41,122; compared with shaman, 89; downgraded, 105; early youth of , 115, 116; entry into Grail Castle, 121; fails question test, 55,58,98,112 118; first awakening, 132; his sister, Dindraine, 105; in Grail Castle, 54-5,76, 121,130; initiation of, 54-5, 117,130,131; in a trance, 89; in composite symbol, 63; in meditation, 81; innocence of, 116; journey of the ego, 102; journey to Sarras, 105; kills bird 53,119,126; leaves Gournemanz, 118; leaves mother, 53; levels of love in, 118; meets and marries Blanchefleur, 54, 118; meets Arthur's knights, 53,116; meets Gournemanz, 54; meets Fisherman, 54; period of despair,55; moves to inner peace, 60; period of penitence, 55,110; *persona* of, 57, 117; quest as rebirth of kingship, 83; rebuilding Temple, 76; revisits Grail Castle, 55,131; sees blood on white background, 92; separation from mother, 116; shadow.of, 117; sits in Perilous Seat, 113; social instruction of, 117-8; spear used by, 83; story in summary, 53-55, 115; tested by Kundry, 128; three stages of story, 116; what his experiences represent, 126; with, angels", 21,116,121
Perfect Man, 62-3
Persian: Mithraic degree, 40,92
Peredur, 16,32,80,93,101-2,114, 116, 134;
Perlesvaus or *The High History of the Grail*, 11,40,93,114,123,124; Joseph of Arimathea in, 114,135; author's probable Temple connections, 22, 114; Grail as shape-shifter in, 11,93; hint of secret tradition in, 93,124; initiatic language in, 22;
"Perfecti" among Cathars, 25,29,93,94
Perfecting Base Metals, 48
Perilous Seat, 103,123,132
Persona, 37,58,117
Personal responsibility, 41
"Petit Saint Graal", 112
Philip, Count of Flanders, 112
Philosophers' Stone, 6,48,49,126
Phrygian mysteries, 96
Phoenix symbol, 15,125
Phrygia, Rituals of, 92,94
Pineal gland, 19,48
"Pog", The, Montségur, 30
"Polars", 121
Portugal, 38
Powell Family, 58
Pre Christian cults, 90
Pre cursors of the Grail, 29

Prehistoric Grail form, 89
Prima materia, 48
Primordial, images, 48
Process of integration, 101
Projected ideal and and real person 118
Projection, 57
Prophecies of Merlin, 136
Proto Grail, 35,89,90
Provence, 40
Pseudo Wauchier, 29,135
Psyche, 55,58,59,67,101,102
Psychic; chaos in Perceval, 60; health, 56 harmony at social level, 56
Psychological and Mystical Perspectives, Ch.12
Psychologists'views of human nature, 103
Puits, 65

Q

Quest: attitudes of quester, 106; failing the mystic, 105,106
Queste del Saint Graal, 21,113,117, 120, 123,126,127,131
Question(s): Perceval's failure to ask, 54,59,66,68,127,128; purpose of, in mysteries, 124,127; we must ask, 60,127; self-examination by introspection, 128

R

Race theory, Hitler's, 83
Rahn, Otto, and Montségur, 31,79; and Nazis, 31; *Kreuzzug gegen den Gral,* 30; in Languedoc, 114
Raven symbol, 93
Ravenscroft, T., 41,50,64,81,94,95
Reality,as One, 105
Reconciliation of opposites, 44
Reconciling religious differences, 125
Redeemer: See "Perceval"
Redemption, 44,126
Red armour, symbolic meaning of, 117
Red Cross, of Templars, 25
Red Knight, 57,58,117; as Perceval's "shadow", 58,117; Galahad as, 117
Reflection, 128
Regression, 87
Reintegration, 44,106
Relationship, 66
Religious attitudes, 39,40; effect on Art, Scholarship,etc.39
Renewal, 66
Repression, 56,84
Repulsive Creature: See "Kundry", Responsibility, 128,129
Return, Myth of, 100
Rites, at Newgrange, 88; of passage 88
River as symbol, 59,119
Robert de Boron, 10,11,21,32,113,122
Rohr, R., 66,67
Role playing, 58
Roman Christianity, 68
Roman legions withdrawn, 68
Roman de la Rose, 51-2
Rose as symbol, 52
Rose Croix, Elder Brothers of the, 25 Rosenkreutz, Christian, 51-2 Rosicrucian(s): activity, 24,25,40; and King symbol, 63; and Templar legacies, 25; archive, 27; Cathars and, 25; as mystics, 84; Grail tours of the, 13,35; ideas in Wolfram's work,17; imagery, 19; modern, 53; nature of organization, 27; the Order in the Great Tradition, 25,93; secret symbols of, 51; temple in London, 25; teachings of, 15; tradition, 25; view of self, 105; visit to Chalice Well, 107
Rosslyn Chapel, 32
Round Table: and Hitler, 83; archetype, 107; collapse of, 107-9; Fellowship of the, 106-7, 111,123; Himmler's,

83; Nazi interest in, 79,83; the next, 107; prophecy of the Perilous Seat, 113; where the Grail search started, 107
Russia, Southern, 70

S

Sabarthez, 31
Sacrament, 84,122
Sacred locations of the Grail, 89
St. Katherine's, Nuremberg, 82
St. Lawrence, 13
Saint Martin, Louis Claude de, 99
Salvation, Views on, 42
San Juan de la Pena, 13
Saracen Knight, 47
Sardinia, 38,105
Sarras, 29,105,123,131
Saxons, 67
Scholarship in Europe, 38-39
Schwarma,48
Second Continuation, 27
Secret(s): gnosis,94; of the Grail, 76, 101, 124,125,126; of the Grail Procession, 124; in Grail Christianity, 40,124; initiation in drama,44; initiatory tradi- -tion, 40-7; of transformation, 19,102; symbols of Rosicrucians, 50; tradition in Europe, 92; of Waste Land, 62
Secret Order, The SS as, 83-4
Segovia, Templar church in, 40
Self: and ego, 62,66,80,101; as archetype, 50,53,62,101,102; as Grail, 50,101; as Perceval and Titurel, 115; definition of, 101; functions of, 101, 102; greater or higher, 83, 104; old and new, 125; redemption of, 101; Rosicrucian view of, 105
Self actualization, 101,103,105; beyond 105
Self realization, 44,106,118,131
Sensual desire, eschewed by Cathars, 92
Separation theme, 73,98,114
Seven degrees of progress, 41,92
"Shadow", The, 56,57,58,117
Shamans, and their experiences, 84-5,111 and "gift", 84
Shape shifting of Grail, 48
Shekinah, 99
Shiz, Parsee sanctuary, 34
Sicily, 38,39
Silbury Hill, 96
Sinclair, A., 29,32
Sinetar, M., 102-3
Siva, Brow of, 19
Snowdonia, Wales, 32,56
Social,discipline, 118; harmony, 90
Solar orientation of Star Temple, 89
Spear or Lance: and Grail in healing process, 75; and Grail as fertility symbols, 96; as axis mundi, 80, 125; as divine will or wisdom, 79, 81; as healer; 129; as intuitive judgment, 79; as phallic symbol, 79; bearer, 126; bleeding, 70,112; caught by Parzival, 123; Celtic, of Lugh, 126; curative properties, 75,79; description of, 81,82; dipped in blood, 59,126; dipped in Grail or cauldron,75,126; diabolical power, 80; divine power of,83; for ego control, 59; Galahad uses it to heal, 78,106; of Destiny, 79, 81; of Lugh, 126; in Grail Procession, 81; in Old Testament 80; magical power of, 79,81,111; masculine ele- ment, 75,124; misuse of, 123,127; of Longinus, 79,81; Perceval uses it to heal,123 sacred and purificatory power, 80 separated from chalice, 83; symbolic value, 75,103; symbol of will or wis- dom,; taken to Heaven, 132; used by Klingsor, 64; used by Perceval, 80; used in meditation, 84; weapon of healing, 11,26; youth as bearer, 124
Society and the Individual, 102
Social attitudes, 73

Socialization, 58
Solar god, 71,92,93
Solar orientation, at Montségur, 93; at Newgrange, 88
Soldier, Intiatic Degree of, 41
Solomon's ship, 105,123,132; temple, 111
Solstice, Temple ceremony at, 76,90,116
Sone of Nansai, 120
Sophia, 74,98; and *vesica piscis,* 108
Soul's journey in Interior Castle, 92
Sources of the Grail Myth, 16,35,89,111, 112
Sovereignty, 42,96,97,101,107
Spain, Moslems in, 38; as meeting point of cultures, 40 tolerance in, 40
"Spectrum of Consciousness", 105,106
Spiral design, 85
Spiritual uplift in the Middle Ages 40
Split(s): God from Creation,65; in personality, 44; Man from God, 65
Sufi mystical practices, 39
Star Temples, 87
Statue of Melchisedek, 27
Stone, The Grail as a, 15,27; Philosophers', 48,49,65; prehistoric basins, 89,90
Stonehenge, 35
Sublimation, 57
Sufi, mystical practices, 39; mysticism and Templars, 17
Sun symbol, 35,52
"Superior people", 104
Swan, and Perceval,119,126,132
Sword, 59,127; as discriminator, 41 59; conferred on worthy,127; conferred as right, 127; different versions of 127;drawn by Galahad and Arthur, 127, magical,111,102; of David 123, of St. Maurice, 101
Symbol(s); chalice and lance, 127; Celtic spear of Lugh;126; forest 115, golden fish, 57; Grail King 62; Grail as alchemical vessel, 124; female as Grail Bearer, 124; fish, 63,108,119; in Book of Lambsprinck, 63; in Callanish Stones 74; in Grail Quest, 41; mountain peak, 121; of blood, 105; of degrees and knights' quest, 93; of Grail King as two persons, 122; of Grail Quest, 94; of lance and negative power, 64; of Mithraic degree, 93; of Mons Philosophorum, 50; of Perceval in the Grail Castle, 131; mother., 115
Symbolic mystical quest, 51-2

T

Tabernacle, 111
Table, Square, 112
Taliesin, 126
Talismans, 111
Tao, 105
Templar Order: activities and repu-tation, 22; and ancient mysteries, 18,92; and Baphomet, 93-4; and Cathar, Rosicrucians, 25; and Crusades, 23; alleged heathen practices, 40,93; aims of, 18; annihilation as Order, 116; as Grail Guardians, 16,22,23; as Knights of the Cross, 40,93; fought against Cathars, 27; in Albigensian Crusade, 25; in Wolfram's Parzival, 15,16,,114; cathedral builders, 22; church in Segovia, 39; founders of; 22; Grail romances and, 31; Grand Masters, 25; guarded Grail Castle, 23; guarded special secret, 23; guardians of esoteric knowledge, 22; in *Der Jungere Titurel*, 23; Nineteenth century interest in, 27; Red Cross symbol of, 25; ritual influenced by Islam, 16,39 92; Rosicrucian connection, 25; sacred rites performed, 23,92; source of strength, 23; symbol at Rosslyn Chapel, 32; "Templeisen" in Parzival, 23;treasure, 23; under-

tones in *Perlesvaus,* 35,93
Temple: chalice Well Garden like open temple,108; establishing harmonies, 87; Neolithic "Star Temples", 89; Templar temple in London,27; point of entry to Otherworld, 89; Solomon's Temple, 73,75
Temporal Round Table, 107
Tennyson, Alfred, Lord, 12,46,127,117
Lady in the Tent, 76
Terrible Mother, 77
Teutonic knights, 23
Third Continuation, 135
Third Eye, 19,49
Third Reich, 79,81,82,83
"Throne of Arches", 34
Tibetan Buddhism, 63
Titurel, 80,83,115; as higher self, 115
Threshold, entering the, 116
Toledo, 15,16,40,48; link with Parzival, 40
Tolerance in Spain, 39
Tor, Glastonbury, 33
Toulouse, 27
Traditio, Cathar preparatory degree, 93
Trance, 116
Transcendence, 130
Transcenders,104
Transcendental alchemy, 16,102
Transcendental level, 104
Transcending: opposites, 102; self, 104
Transformation, 46,92,101,102, 104
Transition to transcendence, 130
Transmutation: See "Alchemy", "Transformation"
Transpersonal, 105
Transpersonal Psychology, 114
Trevrizent, 48,50,89,130
Troubadours and Trouveres, 15,30,40, 41,47,98,102
Troyes, 26
Truth, conveyed by Kundry, 128 Turkey, 70
Turlin, Heinrich von dem, 10

U

Ugly Creature and Gawain,129
Unconscious, archetypal energies of, 120; Celtic Otherworld of the,59; collective, 55,70,101; crossing the threshold of the, 120; equated with feminine, 75; fish as part of, 64; forces of, 66; Grail Myth and the, 70; depths of, 63;
Universal Mind, 105

V

Vegetation myth and ritual, 92,124
Vengeance theme, 80,111
Verbal instruction, 117
Vienna, Hapsburg Museum in, 82
Vesica piscis, 108,119
Virgil, 64
Virgin Mary, 73,76
Vishnu, 63
Visible and invisible worlds, 119
Vivian, 76
Vortigern, 32
Vulgate Cycle, 40,69,112,126,136

W

Wagner, Richard, 12,19,29,44,46,82,83 115,116,,108,126,129,130,133
Wales: Dinas Bran in, 32; Gerald of 32; Rosicrucian Tour of, 32
War in Heaven, 15
Warrior degree, 43,93,135
Waste Land: See also "Grail King"; applicable today, 70; as exile, 98,131; as historical fact, 66; explanations for, 64,66; and Grail King, 62,65,66,67,96; restoring the, 102, 131; symbol of split with God, 65-6
Wauchier de Denan, 130

Wearyhall Hill, 33
Wedding, Alchemical, 52
Wells, Maiden of the, 122
Welsh Perceval, 136
Western mystical path, 106
Weston, J. 41,71,92,94,96,124
Westphalia, Home of Wewelsberg, 83,84
Wewelsberg Castle, 83-4
Whitmont, E.C., 101
Wilber, K., 105
Will, of God, 127; weakness of, 123
Wilmshurst, W., 44,83,127
Winter Dawn Ceremony, 88
Wisdom, *Sophia* as, 74
Wise Old Man archetype, 54,58,117, 130
Witchcraft, 74
Wolfram von Eschenbach; 11,12,15,16, 18,22,40,41,43,48,75,85,103,126,128 and man's condition, 66; and the philosophers' stone, 126; as a cryptic writer, 27; as Hermetic master, 11,12,40,115; as literary alchemist, 47,115; contact with mystery schools, 16; cosmic view of, 44; *Der Junge Titurel*, 136; dualist thought, 115,129; esoteric orientation, 44; Kyot as source of his Grail story, 15,16; lineage factor in Guardianship, 18,114; on the Brotherhood of Mankind, 18; Parzival, 15,18,31,41,48,132,135; referenced by Matthews, 75; reveals Templar connections, 15,16,22,29; shift in Myth's content,15; sources of romance, 40; universal nature of his ideas,15,19; used pseudonyms for real people, 18; used word 'Templeisen', 22
Women: advocate of, 77; as child bearers, 73; as initiatory guides 76; as temptress, 73; confer sovereignty, 78; fulfilment at interior level, 78; Guinevere, 76 impure, 73; initiatory role of, 76; in earlier times, 72; in Celtic and pre Celtic times, 73,74; in the Medieval period, 74; inte-grate life with spirit, 77; Morgan, 77; natural cycles of, 77; need the Quest? 76; not separated from true nature, 77; role in Grail story, 76; status inferiority, 74-5; testing hero, 128; with overcharged masculinity, 77; know secret, 125; quest of, 77
World,War II, 79
Wound, in thigh, 1123; psychic disharmony, 66; of modern humanity, 66
Wounded King: See "Grail King"
Wounded Swan, See "Swan"
Wounding, Sexual, 97

X Y Z

Ynis Witrin, 33
Yogis, 104

Zoroastrian doctrine, 129

THE ROSICRUCIAN ORDER
Its Purpose and Work

Anticipating questions which may be asked by the readers of this book, the publishers take this opportunity to explain the purpose of the Order and how you may learn more about it.

There is only one universal Rosicrucian Order existing in the world today, united in its various jurisdictions, and having one Supreme Council in accordance with the original plan of the ancient Rosicrucian manifestos. The Rosicrucian Order is not a religious or sectarian society.

This international organisation retains the ancient traditions, teachings, principles, and practical helpfulness of the Order as founded centuries ago. It is known as the *Ancient Mystical Order Rosae Crucis,* for popular use, abbreviated to AMORC.

The Order is primarily a humanitarian movement, making for greater health, happiness and peace in people's *earthly lives,* for we are not concerned with any doctrine devoted to the interests of individuals living in an unknown, future state. The Work of Rosicrucians is to be done *here* and *now;* not that we have neither hope nor expectation of another life after this, but we know that the happiness of the future depends upon *what we do today for others* as well as for ourselves.

Further, our purposes are to enable all people to live harmonious, productive lives, as Nature intended, enjoying all the privileges of Nature and all benefits and gifts equally with all of humanity; and to be free from the shackles of superstition, the limits of ignorance, and the sufferings of avoidable *Karma.*

The work of the Order, using the word "work" in an official sense, consists of teaching, studying, and testing such laws of God and Nature as make our members masters in the holy temple (the physical body),and workers in the divine laboratory (Nature's domains). This is to enable our members to render more efficient help to those who do not know, and who need or require help and assistance.

Therefore the Order is a school, a college, a fraternity, with a laboratory. The members are students and workers. The graduates are unselfish servants to humanity, efficiently educated, trained and experienced, attuned with the mighty forces of the cosmic mind, and masters of matter, space and time. This makes them essentially mystics, adepts, and creators of their own destiny. There are no other benefits or rights. All members are pledged to give unselfish service, without other hope or expectation of remuneration than to evolve the self and prepare for a *greater* Work.

The Rosicrucian Sanctum membership program offers a means of personal home study. Instructions are sent regularly in specially prepared lessons, and contain a summary of the Rosicrucian principles with such a wealth of personal experiments, exercises, and tests as will make each member highly proficient in the attainment of certain degrees of mastership. These correspondence lessons and lectures comprise several Degrees.

Each Degree has its own initiation ritual, to be performed by the member at home in his or her private home sanctum. Such rituals are not the elaborate rituals used in the Lodge Temples, but are simple and of practical benefit to the student.

You may receive *a free copy* of the introductory booklet entitled the *Mastery of Life* by writing to:

Scribe "ZGQ, Rosicrucian Order, AMORC
P.O. Box 1087
Burwood North NSW 2134
Australia
or view the Mastery of Life on
www.amorc.org.au

Rosicrucian Library

SELF MASTERY AND FATE WITH THE CYCLES OF LIFE

by H. Spencer Lewis, Ph.D., F.R.C.

This book demonstrates how to harmonise the self with the cyclic forces of each life. Happiness, health, and prosperity are available for those who know the periods in their own life that enhance the success of varying activities. Eliminate chance and luck, cast aside fate, and replace these with self-mastery. Complete with diagrams and lists of cycles.

THE MYSTICAL LIFE OF JESUS

by H. Spencer Lewis, Ph.D., F.R.C.

A full account of Jesus' life, containing the story of his activities in the periods not mentioned in the Gospel accounts, *reveals the real Jesus* at last.

This book required a visit to Palestine and Egypt to secure verification of the strange facts found in Rosicrucian records. Its revelations, predating the discovery of the Dead Sea Scrolls, show aspects of the Essenes unavailable elsewhere. This volume contains many mystical symbols (fully explained) and an unusual portrait of Jesus.

COSMIC MISSION FULFILLED

by Ralph M. Lewis, F.R.C.

This illustrated biography of Dr. Harvey Spencer Lewis, Imperator of the Ancient Mystical Order Rosae Crucis, was written in response to many requests from Rosicrucians and others who sought the key to this mystic -philosopher's life mission of rekindling the ancient flame of Wisdom in the Western world. We view his triumphs and tribulations from the viewpoint of those who knew him best. Recognise, as did Dr. Lewis, that the present is our moment in eternity; in it we fulfil our mission.

MENTAL POISONING: Thoughts That Enslave Minds

by H. Spencer Lewis, Ph.D., F.R.C.

Must humanity remain at the mercy of evil influences created in the minds of the vicious? Do poisoned thoughts find innocent victims? Use the knowledge this book fearlessly presents as an antidote for such superstitions and their influences. There is no need to remain helpless even though evil thoughts of envy, hate, and jealousy are aimed to destroy your self-confidence and peace of mind.

SECRET SYMBOLS OF THE ROSICRUCIANS OF THE 16th AND 17th CENTURIES

This large book is a rare collection of full-size plates of original Rosicrucian symbols and documents. A cherished possession for students of mysticism, this collection includes the Hermetic, alchemical and spiritual meaning of the unique Rosicrucian symbols and philosophical principles passed down through the ages. The plates are from originals and are rich in detail. The book is 30cm by 45cm and is bound in durable textured cover stock.

ROSICRUCIAN PRINCIPLES FOR HOME AND BUSINESS

by H. Spencer Lewis, Ph.D., F.R.C.

This volume contains the practical application of Rosicrucian teachings to such problems as ill health; common ailments; increasing one's income; and how to promote business propositions. It shows not only what to do, but what to avoid, using metaphysical and mystical principles to start and bring into realisation new plans and ideas. Business organisations and business authorities have endorsed this book.

GREAT WOMEN INITIATES The Female Mystic

by Hélène Bernard, F.R.C.

Throughout history, there have been women of exceptional courage and inspiration. Some, such as Joan of Arc, are well known; others have remained in relative obscurity—until now. In this book, Hélène Bernard examines from a Rosicrucian viewpoint the lives of thirteen great women mystics. Her research and insight have unveiled these unsung heroines who, even in the face of great adversity, have staunchly defended freedom of thought and the light of mysticism.

THE MYSTIC PATH

by Raymund Andrea, F.R.C.

This informative and inspirational work will guide you across the threshold of mystical initiation. The author provides insights into the states of consciousness and experiences you may have as you travel the mystic path. It is filled with the fire and paths of the initiate's quest. His spiritual, mental, and physical crises are fully described and pondered. Andrea's deep understanding of the essence of Western mystical and transcendental thought makes this a book you will treasure and refer to often as you advance in your mystical studies. Among the many topics addressed are meditation, contemplation, awakening consciousness, the dark night of the soul, mystical participation, and mystical union.

"UNTO THEE I GRANT..."

as revised by Sri Ramatherio

Out of the mysteries of the past comes this antique book that was written two thousand years ago, but was hidden in manuscript form from the eyes of the world and given only to the Initiates of the temples in Tibet to study privately. It can be compared only with the biblical writings attributed to Solomon. It deals with human passions, weaknesses, fortitudes, and hopes. Included is the story of the expedition into Tibet that secured the manuscript and the Grand Lama's permission to translate it.

THE TECHNIQUE OF THE DISCIPLE

by Raymund Andrea, F.R.C.

The Technique of the Disciple contains a modern description of the ancient esoteric path to spiritual Illumination, trod by the masters and avatars of yore. It has long been said that Christ left a private method for guidance in life as a great heritage to members of his secret council, which method has been preserved until today in the secret mystery schools. The author reveals the method for attaining a greater life taught in these mystery schools, which perhaps parallels the secret instructions of Christ to members of his council. The book is informative and inspiring and splendidly written.

THE TECHNIQUE OF THE MASTER

or The Way of Cosmic Preparation

by Raymund Andrea, F.R.C.

A guide to inner unfoldment! The newest and simplest explanation for attaining the state of Cosmic Consciousness. To those who have felt the throb of a vital power within, and whose inner vision has at times glimpsed infinite peace and happiness, this book is offered. It converts the intangible whispers of self into forceful actions that bring real joys and accomplishments in life. It is a masterful work on psychic unfoldment.

SO MOTE IT BE!

by Christian Bernard, F.R.C.

Explore Rosicrucian views on themes of spirituality and philosophy with Imperator Christian Bernard, whose life has been steeped in the philosophy, heritage, and tradition of AMORC. Each chapter covers a topic near and dear to the soul of students of mysticism, including the power of universal love, the heritage of the Rose-Croix, fear of death, the obscure night, free will, reincarnation, the definition and practice of mystical initiation, and other fascinating topics.

THE SANCTUARY OF SELF

by Ralph M. Lewis, F.R.C.

Are you living your life to your best advantage? Are you beset by a *conflict of desires?* Do you know that there are various *loves* and that some of them are dangerous drives? Learn which of your feelings to discard as enslaving influences and which to retain as worthy incentives. From his years of experience, the author brings you the practical aspects of mysticism.

THE UNIVERSE OF NUMBERS

by Ruth Phelps, F.R.C.

From antiquity, the strangest of systems attempting to reveal the universe has been that of numbers. This book goes back to the mystical meaning and inherent virtue of numbers. It discusses the Qabalistic writings contained in the Sepher Yezirah, and correlates the teachings of Pythagoras, Plato, Hermes Trismegistus, Philo, Plotinus, Boehme, Bacon, Fludd, and others who have explored this fascinating subject.

MENTAL ALCHEMY

by Ralph M. Lewis, F.R.C.

We can transmute our problems to workable solutions through mental alchemy. While this process is neither easy nor instantaneously effective, eventually the serious person will be rewarded. Certain aspects of our lives can be altered to make them more compatible with our goals.

Use this book to alter the direction of your life through proper thought and an understanding of practical mystical philosophy.

MYSTICS AT PRAYER

compiled by Many Cihlar, F.R.C.

The first compilation of the famous prayers of the renowned mystics and adepts of all ages. The book *Mystics at Prayer* explains in simple language the reason for prayer, how to pray, and the cosmic laws involved. You learn the real efficacy of prayer and its full beauty dawns upon you. Whatever your religious beliefs, this book makes your prayers the application not of words, but of helpful, divine principles. You will learn the infinite power of prayer. Prayer, your rightful heritage, is the direct means of communion with the infinite force of divinity.

MANSIONS OF THE SOUL

by H. Spencer Lewis, Ph.D., F.R.C.

Reincarnation, the world's most disputed doctrine! What did Jesus mean when he referred to the "mansions in my Father's house"?

This book demonstrates what Jesus and his immediate followers knew about the rebirth of the soul, as well as what has been taught by sacred works and scholarly authorities in all parts of the world. Learn about the cycles of the soul's reincarnations and how you can become acquainted with your present self and your past lives.

THE INNER WORLD OF DREAMS

by Phyllis L. Pipitone, Ph.D., F.R.C.

Learn all about your dreams and what they can teach you about self and your world. The author takes the reader on a fascinating voyage into a mysterious world in which the dramas of the night can range from the completely outrageous to the lofty and sublime. *The Inner World of Dreams* is written in an easy-to-read style for the beginning and intermediate explorer of the world of dreams. It will give you a good start towards increased insight into your dreams.

THE CONSCIOUS INTERLUDE

by Ralph M. Lewis, F.R.C.

With clarity of expression and insightful penetration of thought, this original philosopher leads us to contemplate such subjects as: the fourth dimension, the mysteries of time and space, the illusions of law and order, and many others of similar import. As you follow the author through the pages into broad universal concepts, your mind too will feel its release into an expanding consciousness.

INSIGHTS

This book presents in a series of essays by various authors, some of the best information on subject of interest to students of mysticism. Some of the subjects included in this book are: what occurs after death, supersight, mystical influence of colour, psychic phenomena, mental creating, self healing, mystery of numbers, Great White Brotherhood and more.

THE GRAIL QUEST: A Search for Transcendence

By Earle de Motte, F.R.C.

Beyond the guise of an earthly search by a noble knight for a lost Grail, there is a much deeper, more profound and mystical meaning to the Grail legend. Here is a profound allegory of mystical initiation, best and most completely understood by sincere students of Rosicrucian and related philosophies.

THE IMMORTALISED WORDS OF THE PAST

compiled by Ralph M. Lewis, F.R.C.

Take a fascinating journey of the mind and spirit as you read these inspired writings. Fifty-eight of the world's most courageous thinkers bring you the benefit of their knowledge and experiences. Each excerpt is accompanied by a biographical sketch of its author. From Ptahotep to Albert Einstein, discover the wisdom of those who pioneered the highest avenues of human expression.

THE WAY OF THE HEART

by Raymund Andrea, F.R.C.

This special edition of sixteen thought-provoking essays includes discussions concerning subjects of particular importance to all people travelling the mystic path. The author encourages every reader to see through the illusions of the modern world so as to experience life's true values. Among the many topics discussed in *The Way of the Heart* are intuitive vs. factual knowledge; the dark night of the soul; the value of scepticism; and group service for improvement of self and humanity. Raymund Andrea's deep understanding of Western mystical and transcendental thought makes this a book you will treasure and refer to often as you advance in your mystical studies.

WHISPERINGS OF SELF

by Validivar

Wisdom, wit and insight are combined in these brief aphorisms that derive from the interpretation of cosmic impulses received by Sar Validivar, the esoteric name of Fr. Ralph M. Lewis, second Imperator of the Rosicrucian Order. These viewpoints of all areas of human experience make an attractive gift as well as a treasured possession of your own.

MYSTICISM THE ULTIMATE EXPERIENCE

by Cecil A. Poole, F.R.C.

An experience is more than just a sensation or a feeling. It is an awareness, or a perception, with meaning. Our experiences are infinite in number, yet they are limited to certain types. Some are related to our objective senses; others to dreams and inspirational ideas. But there is one that transcends them all the mystical experience. It serves every category of our being: it stimulates, it enlightens; it is the ultimate experience. And this book, *Mysticism The Ultimate Experience,* defines it in simple and inspiring terms.

IN SEARCH OF REALITY

by Cecil A. Poole, F.R.C.

This book unites metaphysics with mysticism. It shows us that the human body and its vital phenomenon life are of the same spectrum of energy of which all creation consists. The universe is you because you are one of its myriad forms of existence. Stripping away the mystery of this cosmic relationship increases the personal reality of the self.

SON OF THE SUN

by Savitri Devi

The amazing story of Akhnaton (Amenhotep IV), Pharaoh of Egypt, 1360 B.C. This is not just the fascinating story of one life-it is far more. It raises the curtain on humanity's emergence from superstition and idolatry. Against the tremendous opposition of a fanatical priesthood, Akhnaton brought about the world's first spiritual revolution. He was the first to declare that there was a "sole god." In the words of Sir Flinders Petrie *(History of Egypt):* "Were it invented to satisfy our modem scientific conceptions, his religio-philosophy could not be logically improved upon at the present day."

THE SECRET DOCTRINES OF JESUS

by H. Spencer Lewis, Ph.D., F.R.C.

Even though the sacred writings of the Bible have had their contents scrutinised, judged, and segments removed by twenty ecclesiastical councils since the year AD 328, there still remain buried in unexplained passages and parables the Great Master's *personal* doctrines. Every thinker will find *hidden* truths in this book.

CARES THAT INFEST

by Cecil A. Poole, F.R.C.

With a penetrating clarity, Fr. Cecil Poole presents us with the key to understanding our problems so that we may open wide the door and dismiss care from our lives. The author guides us on a search for *true value so* that, in the poet's words, "the night will be filled with music" as the cares "silently steal away".

ETERNAL FRUITS OF KNOWLEDGE
by Cecil A. Poole, F.R.C.
A stimulating presentation of philosophical insights that will provoke you into considering new aspects of such questions as the purpose of human existence, the value of mysticism, and the true nature of good and evil.

ESSAYS OF A MODERN MYSTIC
by H. Spencer Lewis, Ph.D., F.R.C.
These private writings disclose the personal confidence and enlightenment born of inner experience. As a true mystic philosopher, Dr Lewis shares with his readers the results of contact with the cosmic intelligence residing within.

My Grail Quest Notes

My Grail Quest Notes

My Grail Quest Notes

My Grail Quest Notes